ROC

A Forgotten Mining ~~~

Photo of brick from Rockyside Brickyard
Photo courtesy of George Hines

Thomas W. Zielinsky

with

George B. Hines III

ISBN: 978-0-692-90190-8

Printed by Tri-State Printing Company, Steubenville, Ohio

Front Cover: The first Immaculate Conception Catholic Church built 1904 on Rockyside – Photo courtesy of Dave and Bonnie Burskey

Back Cover: Demolition of the last brickyard – Union plant of Crescent Brick Company – ceased operations in 1980. All kilns eventually will be torn down and hauled away – Photo courtesy of Ed Reese

To Patty

who is always there

with love and support

Thank you for all your help

A Note to Readers

What I truly found amazing while doing research for this book was how many individuals who started brickyard enterprises ended up selling their interests very quickly, sometimes in less than a year. I'm guessing that once the concept of brickmaking took off, individuals appeared out of nowhere, purchased land, built a plant, and started making money.

I couldn't find one single document or official record containing a complete summary of all brickyards. I did find various documents with partial summaries. With documents in hand, I then had to separate and piece information together to make logical sense out of what I was reading. After nearly a dozen documents and records, I was able to create the content of this book. It was very confusing, and often times frustrating, but also exciting at the same time. I certainly hope I got it right.

Also confusing were the dates or years when these brickyards started. These dates varied from document to document; nothing was consistent. If several documents or records represented the same year, then that's the year I used. Realize that some of the information is subjective and might not be the actual date or year of occurrence. The actual plant start dates can be a year on either side of the date given in this book. The information contained herein is as accurate and thorough as the material I had to work with. This process has taken me nearly two years to complete.

As a first example of some of the indifferences, let's examine the Clifton Fire-Brick Works. Some records reference this facility as "Clinton" Fire-Brick Works instead of Clifton. Mr. James S. Porter and Mr. Phillip Beall established this plant in 1836 and worked the facility for seven years. In 1843 Beall rented his interest in manufacturing to Thomas Anderson. Beall passed away in the spring of 1844. The works then became known as T. Anderson & Son, who changed the name to "The Clinton Works."

Then sometime between 1845 and 1850, the works changed hands again to the firm of Mr. Thomas Atkinson & Sons and continued until 1854 when John H. Atkinson purchased all the interests. Atkinson continued to work the property until 1869 when he sold it to Smith, Porter & Company, and it once again became known as the "Clifton Works." We believe this to be the one and same "Clifton Works," and the name difference is a possible spelling error. Since no maps were done doing the early years, it is safe to assume that it truly was a spelling error when information was transferred from one document to another.

As a second example, still with the Clifton Fire-Brick Works, another document stated that sometime around 1856, Mr. Thomas Garlick joined the brickyard started by John H. Atkinson, but under the name of Atkinson & Garlick. A Mr. Thompson Mackey purchased an interest and changed the name to T. Garlick & Company. In 1864, a Mr. Adams purchased an interest, and the name was changed to Atkinson & Adams. Eventually Mr. Adams left to move west, and Atkinson ran the plant alone until 1867 when Cullen & Brothers purchased it. Then it was sold in 1871 to Smith, Porter and Company and became known as the Clifton Upper, Middle, and Lower Works.

With this second example, you can see how confusing the information was in the way it was recorded and the number of times just one brickyard changed ownership or acquired partners. The first document had Smith, Porter & Company purchasing the assets in 1869, and the second document listed the date in 1871. Anyone along the way could have misrepresented years, owners, or a plant name. It is also interesting to note that these various gentlemen didn't start or own an interest in just one brickyard, but invested in several, as the information will describe.

The reader should also know that all of these brickyards were a lot closer to the Ohio River than they are now. In 1900, the Ohio River was much narrower. The Ohio River, at several points below Newell and just north of New Cumberland, was less than a hundred yards wide and had a shallow depth of less than 20 feet. Stories of having the Ohio River actually freeze over, with the ice thick enough you could drive a car across, were once told by my father. In the summer months, depending on how the river shrank, people would swim over to the Ohio side and back.

Today, because of the way our dams have been constructed, the river has gotten wider. Railroad tracks have been moved closer to the highways to allow the rivers to expand. What you will see in the photo section of this book will cause you to wonder.

So, let's get started!

Table of Contents

Acknowledgements

I owe a great debt of gratitude to so many people for all the personal time they gave in helping me put the details into this book. I know I was truly a pain in the backside to Mr. John Kuzio who was so supportive and encouraging upon hearing of my intentions to write about Rockyside. So that's where I begin:

To Mr. John Kuzio (a.k.a. Coach) for your insight and alert memory of what the Rockyside hillside looked like when you were a seven-year old altar server and living at the north end of New Cumberland. From our initial meeting, you knew where all the houses were located and what families lived in those houses. You also told stories of going to school in the one-room Catholic schoolhouse. You kept your mind fresh by sketching various components of Rockyside and the north end of New Cumberland on a piece of onionskin paper. Thank goodness you had the wisdom and foresight to sketch what you remembered on paper.

John, as he wanted me to call him, said I could have the drawing because I was going to need it a lot more than he was. That's where my journey started nearly two years ago.

Unfortunately, John will not see the final outcome of this book, as he passed away at home on February 8, 2017, one day before his 97th birthday. Thank you, my friend, for your great mind, inspiration, and willingness to help with this project.

To my good friend and New Cumberland native Mr. George Hines who helped encourage and motivate me and agreed to co-author this book. Your love of history and your willingness to be part of this project is so much appreciated. Thank you for going with me as we stomped around the hillside looking for clues while getting wacked with branches and blackberry vines and tripping over large dead trees. Keep up your hard work maintaining the history and old pictures of New Cumberland in the New Cumberland City Building.

Thank you to my cousin Ronnie Zumer for your support and historical perspective in maintaining the genealogy of the Zumer family tree. I wish you didn't live so far away, as I certainly could have used your help exploring and covering mile after mile of Rockyside hillside, exploring just like we did up on Newman's hill growing up.

To my cousin Gertrude Ludovici, thank you for your brilliant mind and knowing where buildings, springhouses, the church, and the school were located. Your description of the Rockyside hillside helped me piece it all together. Your knowledge of who had gardens and cows and what each family contributed in support of the other families is so much appreciated.

To a very special lady, who moved away but who I was able to track down and get an exceptional amount of information from, Helen (Spilecki) Brancazio. I'm sorry I called you so many times, but your memory has helped me immensely to put exact detail to the hillside. Thank you for remembering the Union brickyard, the clay incline, and how the boys would ride the clay cars out of the mine on Sunday mornings; this proved invaluable. Thanks too for remembering dances taking place on the Zumer porch on Saturday nights.

Also, a special thank you to Mr. Ed Reese. You have contributed so much to this project, giving of your time, photos, and memories of the families who once lived on Rockyside. Your sharp focus and keen insight, along with a great memory that remembered where those families actually lived on Rockyside, helped verify all the other information. Thank you to Patty, Ed's wife, who helped read, edit, and make final photo suggestions. Your time is also greatly appreciated.

I really can't tell you how many people I've spoken with or received emails from or who directed me to someone they knew who might be able to help, but all the input is so greatly appreciated. To all of you, thank you.

To Dave and Bonnie Burskey. Fortunately, you still read the newspaper. Thank you for seeing my article and deciding to look through an old picture box of your aunt's to find the only picture of the first Catholic Church. Not only a photo of the church but also a class photo of a group of students from the Rockyside School and a photo of the

viii

Rockyside 4H club. Thank you and may God bless you. It truly made this effort worth all our time and energy.

A thank you to the following individuals or businesses for helping us in one way or another to get information, photos, or maps into this book:

Greg Blake – Hancock County Museum
Tina Tate – Hancock County Courier
Virginia McMenamin – Cousin Steubenville, OH
Mike Peterson – Cousin, New Cumberland
Wanda Spilecki – New Cumberland
Jim Caldwell – Wellsburg, WV
Pam and Vito Riggi – New Cumberland
Jon-Erik Gilot – Director of Archives and Records
Wheeling Charleston Dioceses
Pam Haynes – West Virginia Film Office
Vince Schiavoni – President – Duraloy Company
Joe Juszczak– West Virginia Department of Highways
Jim and Bernadette Zucosky – Weirton, WV
Guy Calabro and staff of Newbrough Photo
Dan Tassey – Hancock County Assessor's Office
Steve Trzaskoma – Hancock County Assessor's Office
Vince LaNeve – Hancock County Assessor's Office
Ed LaNeve – East Liverpool, OH
Libraries of: New Cumberland, Weirton, Steubenville, Chester, and East Liverpool
West Virginia Division of Culture & History
West Virginia Department of Mines
United States Library of Congress

Finally, to *Millicent (Milli) Hines*. What can I say? Words cannot express my deep appreciation and gratitude for what you did during the editing process. I will forever be indebted for all you have done. A true godsend at the precise moment in time. Thank you for being a blessed and gifted finicky grammarian, former teacher of French and English; you have enhanced this book immeasurably. Thank you for all your time and your attention to detail. I pray that God will continue to bless and guide you in all that you do.

A Special Dedication

I would like to offer a special dedication of this book to:

Mr. Walter "Peanuts" Czernecki
Daughter – Walena – 13
Son – Domineck - 11

On my first meeting with Mr. John Kuzio,[1] he asked me if I had ever heard of a man called "Peanuts," and I told him, "no." John said he didn't know the man's last name, but he knew and would never forget what happened to him.

Walter and his wife Michalena came from Austria around 1910 and found a home near Congo, West Virginia. Records indicate daughter Walena was born in Congo in 1917. Domineck was born in 1918. Walter worked in the Crescent Brickyard and would later move into a house on Rockyside.

July 18, 1930, proved to be an extremely hotter than usual day, and the kids, who lived on top of Rockyside close to what is now the 911 Center, decided to go for a swim. Apparently Domineck decided to jump into the Ohio River to cool off. Domineck, who was 11 at the time and would turn 12 in just 10 days, was starting to have some difficulty. So, his sister Walena jumped in to try and help Domineck get back to shore, but Domineck started to panic and began pulling his sister farther into the river. On seeing the struggle, Walter jumped in to pull the children out, but he too got caught in the struggle and all three; father age 40, daughter age 13, and son age 11, drowned.

John remembered, upon hearing about the incident, running up from near the Mack Office to the place where the accident happened. Once he got there, all he saw were three bodies lying on top of a pumping shed while the coroner, Mr. G. A. Arner, tended to the bodies. He would not ever forget that image.

All three were laid to rest in the New Cumberland Cemetery on July 21, 1930[2]. No information about Walter's wife (Michalena Sevarcan) could be found.

May their souls rest in Christ's peace

A Special Recognition and Tribute

Mr. John J. Kuzio
February 9, 1920 – February 8, 2017

George Hines and I would be remiss in not paying a special tribute and recognizing Mr. John Kuzio for his tireless effort of wanting us to succeed in getting this book about Rockyside published.

On my first meeting with John, we spent part of the time reminiscing about my days going to New Cumberland High and his coaching ability and the successes he had. He loved sports! He also talked about the successes of his children.

After 30 minutes or so, he showed me an onionskin paper of a drawing that he made over the years, remembering what he could of Rockyside. Incredible detail of houses, tipples, roads, names of families, brickyards, to name a few. Some items were out of place, some being placed on top instead of to the side, but at least he knew what once was there.

As I would receive information, any information, I would call, and he would tell me to come up so he could look at it. My trips to New Cumberland were countless as we processed each piece of information I uncovered.

We would always conclude our visit with stories about his children and grandchildren. His family was everything to him; they made him not only happy, but also extremely proud.

We talked about everything from the war in the Pacific, sports, helping me get the head statistician position at WVU, teaching, family, serving mass every Tuesday, holidays, and Rockyside, especially Rockyside, and all that he remembered about that hillside.

Then, without missing a beat, he got in his car and traveled up to the New Cumberland City Building to discuss everything with George Hines. George was truly a remarkable friend and confidant. He and John were inseparable.

Thank you to a very dear friend. You will be greatly missed.

May you rest in Christ's peace

A Prayer for Guidance

"As I begin this journey, I call upon the Lord to help guide and lead my thoughts and my hand as I begin the writing process. I am led by faith, and I am encouraged and inspired knowing the Lord is with me on this journey."

Thomas W. Zielinsky

"I will instruct you and teach you the way you should go; I will counsel you with my eye upon you."
Psalms 32:8

"A man's mind plans his way, but the Lord directs his steps."
Proverbs 16:9

"I am blessed because I seek refuge and put my trust in the Lord." Psalm 2:1

Introduction
Growing up in New Cumberland

I will always hold a special place in my heart for New Cumberland, West Virginia, where I grew up. I didn't realize what fond and loving memories I had of New Cumberland, until I stood back and was able to do some reflection. This happened in 2006 after I was hired by the Hancock County Commission into a new technology position that was created at the courthouse. Once hired, I began driving back and forth from Weirton and started to once again become familiar with certain landmarks of the town that I had forgotten. I started feeling sentimental and a little nostalgic realizing that I really missed this "one-horse" little town where I grew up.

I realized it was an honor and privilege to grow up in New Cumberland in the 1950's, and will always consider this town home. New Cumberland was where it all started for me; where I made friends, played ball, went to school and to dances at the library, where I attended church, and sat on the bank corner in the evenings. I left town when I was 18 years old. Growing up in New Cumberland, I learned respect; first and foremost. First to your parents; clergy; relatives (aunts and uncles); legal authority (police, justices of the peace, constables, judges); neighbors; and anyone you came in contact with. You better be polite and respectful. Mr. or Mrs. or sir or madam, were the first words out of my mouth. If you didn't, then there were consequences, serious consequences.

Children growing up today have no concept of what it was like growing up in the 50's. We had none of the so-called conveniences of today. No cell phones, iPads, computers, calculators, Xboxes, CD players, iPod's; no nothing. A "slide rule" was my calculator. Our only convenience was a very awkward-looking radio that measured nearly four feet tall.

This large, wooden-frame tube radio, called a Sparton, received a ton of stations, even short wave, and stood against the wall in our living room. After dinner and having our homework finished, we would listen to various radio programs just before going to bed. Programs like "Amos and Andy,"

"Abbot and Costello," "The Shadow," "The Lone Ranger," and the list goes on. How great it was listening and letting your imagination create a picture from what was being said. We would sit on the floor directly in front of the big radio speaker with large pillows.

Those same pillows would later be used to watch TV. We got our first TV in 1952. It was a 21-inch black and white RCA Victor, with "rabbit ears" for an antenna. We eventually got an outside antenna so we could make the picture a little clearer. Funny thing about TV back then was it came on at 6 in the morning and signed off at 11 at night – can you imagine? But the worst was only receiving two channels; 7 from (Wheeling) and 9 from (Steubenville). Some of our neighbors, in addition to channels 7 & 9, received channels 2 and 4 out of Pittsburgh, but that required a special antenna that had to be located high on the hill from where we lived, known as New Cumberland Heights.

Reflecting on my past, growing up in New Cumberland was an exceptional experience for me. Very few people today, unless you actually grew up in a small town, will ever understand what a small-town experience is all about. What stands out the most were the people. Everyone looked out for one another, including us kids. Even the police kept a keen eye on everything we did, and you better not be doing anything wrong, because they would tell your parents. Strong family values were part of what made growing up so special. Mom and dad would always extend help and sharing to anyone in need, and I learned from their example. We did everything together as a family, especially Sunday drives to get ice cream, and then a visit to grandma's house.

My memories of growing up started with two very hard-working parents who provided what they could for their children. Their work ethic helped me to develop a similar style, which has helped me all through my life. My motto is "work hard, always do your best, and you won't be disappointed."

A number of years ago I found a saying in the comic strip by *Plato from Beetle Bailey* that said, "Don't expect something for nothing. A man is worth what a man does!" I have always tried to live by those words of wisdom.

2

Dad worked turns in the mill, so he wasn't home much, but then there was mother who helped fill the void. What an exceptional woman who did the shopping, cleaned the house, helped with our homework, and managed to create the most amazing meals and pies. A mother who wanted more for her children and often sacrificed things for herself. She was a kind person who would radiate warmth and love; not only for her family, but also to everyone she met. It was that warm and comforting feeling I remember most. The feeling isn't hard to describe. It was a feeling of having loving arms surrounding your body, arms ever so gently squeezing warmth all through you. That feeling of warmth usually was needed more on dark and rainy days or dark and snowy days.

I remember walking home from school, especially in the fall and winter months, with the smell of burning coal and watching smoke coming out of every chimney in sight. It's a smell you don't find anymore since coal furnaces when out in the 60's. But smelling that scent and walking into a warm home was so, so comforting.

I attended a one-room schoolhouse for my first three years, which I found truly amazing. A Catholic school that started in 1921 sat next to the bank of the Ohio River with railroad tracks located just outside the front door. What an experience. We had no running water in the building, only a well in the center courtyard which provided our drinking water, two outside toilets (his and hers), and one large potbelly coal stove between two classrooms. Water was poured in a large metal container in the center hallway. Everyone brought a plastic glass from home with a piece of tape with your name on it. These were kept on a tray next to the water dispenser. The glasses were cleaned about once of month, if we were lucky.

The school was just adjacent to the second Catholic Church built on the corner of North Chester and Jackson Streets. In those days, little concern was given to heating the church. Body heat from the person next to you was hopefully enough. I still remember going to church in the winter with my mother for evening rosary service, which we only recited in Polish, and coming out not being able to feel my toes.

The heat source in houses back then was traditionally a coal furnace with hot water radiators under the windows. The

3

coal was used to heat a large boiler filled with water. Water was then forced up and through the radiators and then returned to the boiler to be reheated. Anyone who has seen *A Christmas Story* knows all too well what a "clinker[1]" is. You didn't have a coal furnace without getting a clinker from time to time. In the mornings, mother would place a large towel over the rough ridges on top of the radiator. It would get nice and warm for us to sit on while we dressed for school.

Our years growing up were all based on keeping our Polish tradition, especially at Christmas and Easter. On Christmas Eve, the entire family would go to Grandma Zielinsky's house for a dinner called Wigilia, pronounced (vee-geel-ya), which stands for Christmas Eve. Once the dinner was over, the adults would prepare to attend midnight mass, with caroling (in Polish), but for the rest of us, it was getting home and ready for bed because Santa was on his way.

Christmas meant we had to get up really early so we could check what Santa brought us before getting dressed and going to church. After church, mother would always prepare a turkey dinner with all the trimmings. Then instead of getting to play with your new toys, we had to get ready to go visit the relatives. For those relatives that were close by, we just walked, whether up or down the hill. For other relatives, we had to take the car. Trying to get in five or six homes in a day was a real effort. By the time you came home, you were too tired to even look at your toys. For several days after Christmas, the families we visited were now obligated to come visit our house. So we had company for two or three days after Christmas, which meant we still didn't have much time to play with our toys. Then Christmas vacation was over, and back to school.

Easter was essentially the same thing, but consisted of three holy days leading up to Easter during which preparations needed to be made. It wasn't like Christmas, but it was still exciting and concluded with mother's turkey dinner with all the trimmings. Since Easter didn't require visits to the relatives, I always preferred toys at Easter so we could enjoy them more. But, we so enjoyed our traditions.

The one thing we all did, the young and old alike, was walk. And we walked everywhere – to school, to church, to the store, to downtown, to the ball field, to Second or Third

Avenue to visit friends; we walked everywhere. My cousin Ronnie Zumer and I probably logged a couple hundred miles walking our hillside, over the pasture of the Stewart farm, down Cemetery Hill Road to visit our deceased relatives in the cemetery, then walking out Hardins Run Road to the once natural spring for a drink of water, before turning around to head back home.

When I was about ten, my dad bought me my first bike. It was only a 24-inch model since I was so short, but it got me where I need to go a lot quicker than walking. By the time I was fourteen, I outgrew it and then went back to walking. Dad, for some reason, didn't see the need to get me a larger bike.

After our priest, Father Olszewski passed away in 1955, they closed the Catholic school and everyone now had to attend New Cumberland public school. Public school opened up so many more exciting experiences for me. My first day was in fourth grade with probably the most amazing teacher of my life, Mrs. Campbell. (Her full name was Margaret "Sis" Campbell. She lived to be 96.) What an amazing teacher! Remembering Friday afternoons with "Jane and I" still brings back how she would capture and sweep our minds away for an hour into a magical land of make-believe with her stories about her friend Jane and their amazing adventures. No script, no notes, truly all from the heart. I so miss those stories.

I loved the fourth grade because it was there that I saw and met the most beautiful girl in the world sitting just a few rows from where I was sitting. When I looked at her, all kinds of flip-flops started in my stomach, and I felt light headed. My next-door neighbor, after finding out that I had a crush on this girl, invited me to a play at the Presbyterian Church where she was going to perform. For an hour, I was in my glory. We became good friends all though school, but it wasn't until I was about to come out of the Army that we actually went out on our first date. She is still as beautiful today as she was when she was nine. Although our lives took different directions, every time I see her, those funny feelings from the fourth grade come rushing back. *Boy, what a great school. Nothing like Catholic School!*

Going to school was now twice as long because we no longer ran down over our hill to the main road (North

5

Chestnut Street) crossed past the Catholic Church, and then crossed the railroad tracks and into school. We now had to go down Newman's Hill, past the A&S Food Store, walk the path along the creek to what is now New Cumberland City Park, cross over a wooden bridge, and walk up a gravel hill (I know the reason for the school's name) to the school. That was in the morning. We would repeat that three more times. Walk home for lunch, then back to school, and then walk home after school. Walk, walk, walk. But we didn't seem to mind.

All the kids living in town had to walk to school. Kids from upper town or Second or Third Avenue had the really long walks. Only the kids that lived outside of town were privileged to ride a school bus.

What really killed me was taking my accordion to school to perform in school functions. I probably weighed no more than 65 pounds and carried a 25-pound accordion back and forth over that same terrain. *Boy, that was tough.*

As I got a little older and showed that I was responsible to be on my own, mom or dad would give me money to go to the movies at the Manas Theater. I can still see Bill at the counter and his wife Nellie in the booth or sometimes vice versa. With two dollars, you could see a movie, get a square of pizza and a small drink, and get back change.

I lived on Newman's Hill (Commerce Street was the proper name) where most of my mother's family lived. Her one sister and brother were just across the street. Two sisters lived directly over the hill from us. With all my cousins close, we always had someone to play with. My dad's family home was on North Chestnut Street. They had an adjacent piece of land they used for gardening. Every summer we'd have someone come with a very large tractor to plow and smooth the dirt, and then my dad, his brother, and a couple of brothers-in-law would do the planting. Then every fall would come the picking and canning. We always had a very large assortment of canned fresh fruits and vegetables that mother would use all winter.

Newman's Hill was an exceptionally beautiful place to live, not just because we were close to our relatives, but because everyone took such great care of their homes and lawns and had flowers growing everything. We had a small turn-around area just out the road from our house, which was

6

located at the ridge of an old garbage dump. In the early days, before trash pickups, everyone just pitched it over the hill into this very wide ravine. This is the area where we played ball almost every day. I can tell you it was "hell" going down in all that garbage to get our ball, because we either missed a catch or fouled one over our makeshift backstop. But it kept all of us "on-the-hill" and in shouting distance of our mothers.

There was a total of nine families on this hill; as you came up the hill, the very first homes on the right were the families of:

McKitrick (Dean, wife Edna, and children; Dena, Gloria, Debbie, Tom, and John David),
Lohr (Jim, wife Mary and children; Marion, Mildred, Eleanor "Sis"),
Zumer (John, wife Mary and children; Mary Ann, Richard, and Ronnie),
Knight (Oral, wife Verna and children; Nancy, Charlotte, and Donald),
Kiger (Bill, wife Wilma and son; Wayne) – lived all the way at the end of the road pass the dump.

On the left side coming up the hill were the families of:

Clark (Virginia, lived alone),
Ryan (Ethel, no husband and son Lawrence),
Zielinsky (Walter, wife Walda and children; Tom, John, and Donald),
Gehring (George "Dutch", wife Francis and children; George "Ronnie", Pam, and Sally).

These families lived on the hill even after their children moved away. Some families moved, while other families would continue to live out their lives there. Everyone looked out for all of us kids, and we had better not be doing anything that would lead to a belt having to be used. I always tell people that if my parents were alive today, they would both be in jail because of the beatings. But the irony is we all grew up and became responsible adults.

The winters on Newman's Hill were always great. If we didn't have school, which wasn't very often, and a large snow fell, we would spend hours packing the hill for sled riding. Each kid was fortunate to have his own sled, so we would all take turns to see how far our sleds would take us. On a good day, we could come past the A&S Food Store. Then the long hike back up the hill, dragging that sled and trying not to get run over by those coming down the hill. We would be out all day, except if mother called, to get us drier cloths or something to eat. Sometimes we would build a fire at the bottom of the hill, if cars weren't parked there. We would get the hill so packed it would take days before a car could come up the hill without risking sliding into the hillside.

I wanted to write this book to capture some of my memories of growing up in New Cumberland so others could share my experiences. But once I started doing some family background gathering, I realized this was bigger than I imagined. All of my grandparents arrived from different parts of Europe and all settled in New Cumberland, but not just New Cumberland, they settled first on Rockyside. This is where their families all started.

But like everything in life, things fade away and are soon forgotten. Like Rockyside, the families that once lived and worked on that hillside have all faded into the sunset. Maybe just a few family members might still be around to remember, but most is forgotten. Everything is slowly fading away.

I left New Cumberland in August of 1964 only to return 42 years later in 2006. After I was here for several months, it really dawned on me that the town of New Cumberland was also fading away. Newman's Hill is nearly gone; overgrown with weeds and trees, some homes completely crumbled in piles, others uninhabitable, some in desperate need of repair, and only four families now live there. The beautiful lawns, flowers, shrubs and trees are all gone, as are the original families. Everything is fading away.

The same process is happening to the town with only a few of the original buildings still standing. Some buildings have become worn and are crumbling, while others are gone completely. Streets have changed, houses have burned and been plowed under, complete structures eliminated, with the entire fabric of what I remembered about New Cumberland quickly fading away.

But for me, while there are still a few people left, I decided to capture a fleeting moment in time and reclaim what I could of Rockyside and what it once looked like. There are no pictures, only memories, of this hillside where it all began. I will try and recreate a picture of what that hillside looked like for the next generation.

As I started on this journey, I quickly realized that so many people had never heard of Rockyside or even knew that it ever existed. The exceptions, of course, were people like me who had a parent or relative who once lived there before moving into the town of New Cumberland.

As I began searching for information about Rockyside, I came to realize there was no information anywhere. No one ever took time to document this amazing hillside. There were several books written about Hancock County that went into some detail about how the brickyards and brickmaking started, but nothing about Rockyside, the community. So, this became my quest.

I started my journey with nothing more than a DVD video my father made in 1994. One piece of information led to another until a picture started to form. It's been like trying to piece together a jigsaw puzzle but without having a picture to guide you along.

As fragmented as the data is and how some data contradicts other data, I wanted to create an accurate account of brickmaking and clay mining in New Cumberland. But most importantly, I wanted to recreate what Rockyside and that forgotten hillside community actually looked like over 100 years ago.

This book is for future generations to look back and say, "New Cumberland made its mark on the world, and I'm proud to have grown up in New Cumberland."

One of several favorite Christmas movies of mine is, "It's a Wonderful Life." It's a movie that represents one man seeing what the world would be like if he hadn't existed; how one life touches the lives of so many other lives. Like George Bailey, we sometimes don't fully appreciate what we have or what we've accomplished. New Cumberland as a town, as a community, has touched so many other towns and communities all across the globe, but few realize the significant contribution this town has truly made to the world.

Bricks from this community are in steel mills all over the world, and on streets and in towns we'll never know. Stainless steel cutlery from this community is currently all over the world as well; in homes, hotels, and restaurants that we'll never know. China and glassware of a specific design and category, made in this community, are in parts of the world we'll never know. New Cumberland has contributed more to the world than we know or could ever appreciate. It all started here in the little town of New Cumberland, West Virginia, many, many years ago.

Follow with me as I uncover not only the brickyards and clay mines, but also my family's background through the first generation. What I remember most about growing up in New Cumberland – this is a great town, a great community, with great people, and a great place to live. For my family and me it all started on Rockyside. So, here we go!

Chapter One
Brickmaking in New Cumberland

The history of brickmaking in New Cumberland began around 1832, even though New Cumberland didn't become established until 1839. In those early years, around 1830, the mining of clay began. Known as Kittanning fire clays, they were mined near the mouth of Holberts Run and shipped by barge to brickyards in Pittsburgh, PA.[1] In 1839 when New Cumberland was formally established, New Cumberland was considered the largest brick-manufacturing center in the state of West Virginia.

After realizing how much clay was available, opportunists James Porter and Thomas Freeman decided brickmaking could be a lucrative business. In 1832, just two years after clay mining began, the very first brick plant was being constructed and became known as Freeman's Brickyard. In the following twelve years, five additional brickyards were established in the town, and the production in 1837 was 200,000 bricks[1] just for the Pittsburgh market.

Soon after the first brickyard was erected, another brickyard was started by Thomas Freeman in 1834, one mile and a half below New Cumberland. It was called the Claymont Fire Brick Company until sometime around 1890. In 1897, this brickyard became the T. J. Garlick and Company – Brick and Tile Works, and around 1902 it was purchased by the Porter Company. They, in turn, changed the name back to the Claymont Brick and Tile Works. It remained Claymont until around 1942 when it was finally torn down.

Around 1837, two other brickyards were being built; Lone Star Brick Works just north of the mouth of Kings Creek was built but didn't start operating until 1845. The Sligo Brick Company just north of the Lone Star plant and south of Zalia, was owned by the Standish Brick Company. Both of these plants were initially started by James Porter and Phillip Beall, and then the companies switched hands.

11

In 1845, Mr. McCoy and Mr. Shawl sold their interests in the Clifton Works to Thomas Atkinson & Sons (John H. and Alexander). Around this time, Cooper and Brothers started another plant south of the mouth of Kings Creek that began as Cooper, Gay, and Company. It was later sold to Mr. Campbell & Mr. Logan, who finally sold it to Smith, Porter, and Company.

The Clifton Works had a name similar to another company that was started by James Porter and Phillip Beall in 1836 as the Clifton Fire Brick Company. It was built just north of New Cumberland in 1836, beginning as a small brickyard, but with the capacity to expand.

During the period between 1837 and 1844, Thomas Freeman, James Porter, and Phillip Beall supplied the entire brick market. Bricks were placed on keelboats that could carry upward of 20,000 bricks and travel to Pittsburgh and Wheeling. These boats were loaded near the mouth of Holberts Run at a placed called Freeman's Landing. It took about three days with horses towing carts to load just one boat.

Mr. Phillip Beall died in the spring of 1844, and Mr. James Porter took ownership of his assets and began building another brickyard just north of the Sligo plant along with Thomas Anderson. This plant became known as Anderson Brothers Brick and Sewer Pipe Works in 1848. The first plant on this spot was built three years earlier by gentlemen known only as Kerr and Mahan, who ended up selling their plant and assets to John Porter and Thomas Anderson and Company.

Around 1846, Mr. Shanley and Mr. Flowers opened a new brickyard above the sawmill owned by Jeremiah Smith located on Hardins Run Road. Then, Mr. Carson and Mr. Minn opened another brickyard about half a mile farther up Hardins Run, near what was known as the Williamson's sawmill. These two brickyards were a long distance from the Ohio River, which limited their trade and shipping, causing the owners to abandon the businesses. Their machinery was later removed to more convenient sites.

In 1845, the area north of New Cumberland was being looked at for new development opportunities since the land between Holberts Run and the mouth of Kings Creek was already saturated with brickyards and sewer pipe facilities. Mr. Joseph Stewart started an unnamed brickyard in 1840 near the mouth of Deep Gut Run just north of New Cumberland and put the plant in operation in 1844, partnered with his son-in-law Mr. Hugh Muntz. Upon the death of Mr. Stewart, Thomas Atkinson became one-third owner along with Smith, Porter, and Company. The firm became known as Atkinson, Porter, and Company.

James and William Porter didn't sit idle, but began investing and preparing plans for plants in an area just north of Deep Gut Run known as the Aetna (Etna) and the Cunningham plants. Meanwhile, James & William Porter, Mr. James Freeman, Mr. Kerr, and Mr. John Mahan started building a new brick and sewer pipe plant just south of New Cumberland in 1845. (John Mahan was the father-in-law of Captain John Porter.) This plant eventually changed its name to the Black-Horse Works. It was about at this same time the Sligo plant began installing equipment to begin making sewer pipe.

The firm of James and William Porter continued through 1848 when the firm added Mr. B. J. Smith as a partner. In 1851, William sold his interest to Robert Porter, who then became a partner, and the firm changed its name to James S. Porter & Company. James S. Porter retired in 1867, and the firm became Smith, Porter, & Company.

In 1851, Mr. Alfred H. Chapman started the Chapman Foundry at the south end of Commerce Street in New Cumberland. Many years later in 1944, Matthew Phillips would purchase the foundry.

Plants continued to be built, and names continued to change. In 1853, the Aetna plant was purchased by Thomas Manypenny along with brothers Joseph, Alexander, and John, and they changed the spelling of the name to just Etna.

No strangers to the brick business, John H. Atkinson and Thomas Garlick started another brickyard in 1856, about two miles south of New Cumberland that became known as American Fire Brick Company. Two years later in 1858, Thomas Garlick with Thomas and John H. Atkinson started the Crescent Brickyard Plant just north of the Clifton Works. Crescent Brick started under the name of Middle and Upper Clifton Works, with Crescent being the Upper plant.

In that same year, the Freeman plant became operational near the mouth of Holberts Run. This plant was started by James, Samuel, and Charles Freeman and became known as the Freeman & Brothers Plant.

Thomas Manypenny, owner of the Etna plant, began building a new plant in 1868 and named it the Union Brickyard plant. The very next year, John Atkinson, who owned the majority of the Clifton Works, sold his interests to Smith, Porter, and Company. However, he did not include the Crescent plant in the sale.

In 1870, John Manypenny along with George Cuppy started yet another brickyard one-half mile north of the Etna plant known as the Eagle Works. This plant would later just make sewer pipe. After a short time, Mr. Cuppy sold his interests to John T. Robb, who left for California, selling his interests to Cunningham, Graham, and Company. During this same period, Isaac Evans and F. Shane entered into partnership and began building the Rockyside Brickyard plant.

Just a few years later, in 1874, Mr. David Troup purchased property just north of the Rockyside plant and began building another plant partnering with Mr. James Porter. Initially known as the Standard Fire Brick Company, it was located roughly three miles north of New Cumberland at the bottom of a long hill. The plant would eventually be changed to the Globe Brick Plant, and the hill would be known as Globe Hill Road.

Another new plant sprang up in 1880 and was known as the Cunningham plant, or the Cunningham and Taylor Brickyard. Mr. Cunningham and Mr. Taylor partnered to build this facility, although the initial plans for this facility were made years earlier by James and William Porter. The plant was completely destroyed by fire in 1881.

In 1889, the Black-Horse Works was sold to the American Sewer Pipe Company, and in the very next year Mr. John Porter, a.k.a. Captain John Porter, began his run purchasing brickyard assets. He already owned the Union, the Etna, and the Eagle brickyards by 1890. Three years later, he continued his acquisition of brickyards by purchasing 35 acres of property just south of Newell, WV, on which he built Kenilworth Brickyard. This plant would eventually become Globe Brick Company.

Captain John Porter sold all his brickyard assets in 1894 to the Mack Manufacturing Company of Philadelphia, PA, partnered by Mr. John P. Mack and Mr. A. N. Servall. These assets included Rockyside, Union, Eagle, and Etna, as well as all of Clifton, Crescent, and Sligo brick and sewer pipe facilities. Officers of the company were: president – A. N. Servall, treasurer and general manager – John P. Mack, and secretary and manager of factories – S. G. Gaillard. Eventually these plants would be consolidated for the final time under the name of the Crescent Brick Company. But this change did not come about until 1924.

Newcomers Mr. Charles W. and N. W. Ballantyne started the West Virginia Fire Clay Manufacturing Company in 1896. Two years later, they would change the name to West Virginia Fire Clay Company. The sole purpose of the company was to crush and refine clay, and the plant remained operational until 1948.

In 1901, Alfred H. Chapman, who began the Chapman Foundry, established the Acme Clay Works at the same location as the foundry at the south end of Commerce and Straight Streets in New Cumberland.

After such a flurry of new factories, building seemed to slow down. In 1904, the Mack Manufacturing Company closed the Clifton Works, Sligo, and Eagle facilities. The Eagle was the first to close, followed a year later by both the Sligo and Clifton plants. In 1907, the Etna plant was destroyed by fire, but it was eventually rebuilt. In 1911, the Union Brickyard was also destroyed by fire and eventually rebuilt.

Sometime between 1904 and 1906, the Globe Brick plant at the north end of New Cumberland was completely destroyed by fire and never rebuilt. However, in 1909, the new Globe Brick Yard was incorporated and placed in full production by Captain John Porter. This plant manufactured paving bricks and was family owned until acquired by Combustion Engineering of Stamford, Connecticut, in 1970. The name was then changed to Globe Refractories. Globe brick had attained the status as the world's most highly automated pouring pit refractories plant and the largest ladle brick plant in America serving the steel industry. Globe Refractories closed sometime in the 1980's.

The Mack Manufacturing Company, after acquiring new assets, hired S. G. Gaillard, an experienced railroad and mining engineer, as superintendent and manager of its entire works. Mack felt the supply of clay would soon be exhausted, and Gaillard's first assignment was to locate new clay mines. After an intense search, he found new mines from both the Clarion and Kittanning veins. He immediately began automating the plants by enlarging and modernizing the kilns. Automatic cutters were installed, and production increased with fewer employees. In 1912, he purchased two steam shovels, the first for the brickyard, along with new crushers and mechanical sledgehammers. Drying tunnels were enlarged, and huge Corliss engines and additional boilers were utilized. These improvements were completed in 1916 at enormous costs.

After all these improvements, the Mack Manufacturing Company decided to sell all of its holdings to Wheeling Capital under the leadership of Mitchell and Stevenson, Inc. About 1920, Mr. Gaillard severed his connection with the company.

When Mr. Gaillard severed his relationship with the Mack Company, a Mr. T. C. Steveson of Wheeling was hired on. During this period, only the Rockyside, Union, Etna, and Crescent brickyards were in operation. Coal prices were highly elevated, and exorbitant freight charges caused some loss of business to distant markets, which constituted one-half of Mack's business.

So, to remain competitive, Steveson added electricity to the coal mines and clay mines for drilling as well as for light. He constructed new coal chutes, utilized truck tractors to transport coal from the chutes to the kilns and boilers, installed a clay hoist at Crescent, and built a ground clay bin and clay feeder to insure maximum and uniform production.

Then in 1924, Mr. W. A. Bonitz of Pittsburgh purchased the remaining brickyard assets and changed the name of the group of companies to a single name, the Crescent Brick Company. Upon his death in 1926, Mr. D. D. Moses purchased the company, and Mr. D. Robert Ferguson, Jr., was selected president. Crescent closed all operations in 1980.

In 1944, Mr. Matthew Phillips of the Matthew Phillips Company purchased the Chapman Foundry. This foundry had relocated into New Cumberland at Taylor and South Chester Streets. He used this site for his new businesses. The Phillips Company was a holding company with three divisions; New Cumberland Metal Products which consisted of manufacturing highway forms and accessories, steel fabricating, television and radio parts and making snow tools; Phillips Hardware and Supply Company founded in 1947; and Phillips Lumber and Supply Company founded in 1952. He also operated the Phillips Coal and Clay Company and M&E Company with his son Edward L. Phillips.

Measuring Distances and Determining Locations

It was fascinating to learn how brickyards were classified as to their relative locations in Hancock County. There were actually two different ways, which was a little confusing at first. Some sources used the north and south city limit markers of New Cumberland as a reference. However, I was able to get a better sense of location by using Sanborn Fire Insurance Maps.

Sanborn Fire Insurance Maps is an American publisher of historical and current maps of US cities and towns. Sanborn maps were originally created for assessing fire insurance liability to urbanized areas in the United States. The maps were initially created to estimate fire insurance risks and actually date back to 1866. The company's maps are frequently used for historical research and for preservation and restoration efforts. Sanborn's insurance map business began to decline after World War II, as the insurance industry began modernizing methods of assessing and mitigating risk. The Sanborn maps themselves are large-scale lithographed street plans at a scale of 50 feet to one inch (1:600) on 21" by 25" sheets of paper. All maps that I was able to acquire were through the Library of Congress. An original printed to scale map is hanging in the New Cumberland City Building.

The Sanborn Fire Insurance Company maps, for consistency, used the town courthouse as a center or reference point for all measurements. As an example, the Clifton Works was referenced as a location one mile north of New Cumberland. The actual location was approximately less than a quarter mile from the northern city limits marker. However, when measured from the courthouse, it would be exactly one mile. I have included a chart showing both actual measured distances and those represented by the Sanborn Maps.

Distances I reference in this book are from the city limit markers, not the Sanborn distances.

The location chart which follows shows where all brickyards were located, both south and north of the town of New Cumberland, for the years 1890 and 1897. This chart shows both mileage distances using city limit markers and the Sanborn Insurance Map distances using the courthouse as a reference marker. All distances are measured in miles.

Location chart of Brickyard facilities in New Cumberland

Mileage Distances	Sanborn Distances	Brickyard Plants Year 1890	Brickyard Plants Year 1897
2.5 S	3.25 S	Lone Star Works	Lone Star Works
2 S	2.75 S	Sligo Fire Brick	Sligo Fire Brick
1.75 S	2.5 S	Anderson Bros	McElfresh Clay
1.5 S	2.25 S	Claymont	T.J. Garlick
1.25 S	2 S		Freeman Plant
.75 S	1.75 S	Original Freeman	N.W. Ballantyne
.25 S	1.25 S	McMahan, Porter	Black-Horse
-	.75 S	Chelsea China	Chelsea China
-	.5 S	NC Glass Works	NC Glass Works
0	0	*New Cumberland City Limits*	
.25 N	1 N	Clifton Fire Brick	Clifton Sewer Pipe
.5 N	1.2 N	Crescent Brick	Crescent Brick
.75 N	1.4 N	Aetna Fire Brick	Etna Fire Brick
.85 N	1.5 N	Cunningham	----
1.25 N	1.8 N	Eagle Fire Brick	Eagle Sewer Pipe
1.5 N	2 N	Union Fire Brick	Union Fire Brick
1.75 N	2.25 N	----	Rockyside
2.25 N	2.75 N	Globe Fire Brick	Globe Fire Brick

The following map example is from the Sanborn Insurance Maps Company, dated 1897, for the first brickyard, one mile and a half south of New Cumberland. In 1897, it was called T. J. Garlick & Company Brick and Tile Works. This plant was started initially as the Claymont Plant of Porter Brick Company and began in 1834. These maps were quite detailed and provided a wealth of information. Notice the difference between using town marker and courthouse measured distances.

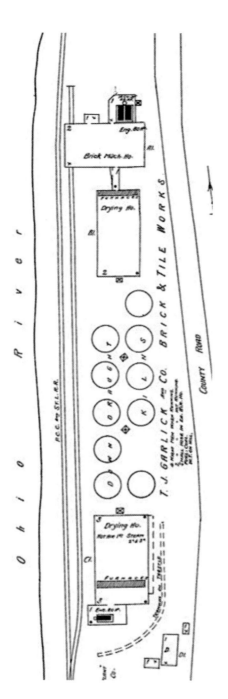

Sanborn Insurance Map 1897 of T. J. Garlick & Company formally started as the Claymont Plant owned by American Fire Brick[4]

Chapter Two
Location of Rockyside

So where exactly is Rockyside, West Virginia? When I started my research, it was difficult (to say the least) to ask anyone from New Cumberland if they knew where Rockyside was located. So many people either didn't remember or said they had never heard about Rockyside or even knew it existed.

If you try to "Google" Rockyside, all you get is a reference to Rockyside Road or County Highway 66/1 New Cumberland with a point near the J. D. Rockefeller Center just north of town.

Rockyside is also displayed two separate ways; Rocky Side as two words, or Rockyside as one word. The one word representation is used in most of the research material I found, so I will continue to spell Rockyside as one word.

My next journey was to find any evidence of Rockyside on any map anywhere. The earliest map I found was a map from 1852 titled *The Map of Hancock County Virginia.* This of course was before we became the great state of West Virginia. However, there was nothing printed on that map that indicated where Rockyside was located.

I found maps from 1871 and 1906, but no reference to Rockyside. Then I got lucky and came across a map dated 1924[1] that actually showed Rockyside, and interestingly enough, markers for a school and a church. This information came to me from the Hancock County Assessor's Office. This map was exactly what I needed to show that Rockyside did exist at one point in time.

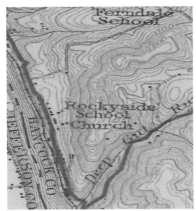

Rockyside shown on WV Geological Survey Map 1924

As you see in the photo on the left, Rockyside sits between Deep Gut Run to the south and Ferndale School to the northeast. The road leading up to the Ferndale School just happens to be named Rockyside Road. The photo on the right indicates (bottom circle) a small + where the church is located and (top circle) a small dot where the school is located. Just to the left of the circles is a series of black dots that indicate where homes were located along the east side of Route 66. What a great find, thanks again to the Hancock County Assessor's Office.

Rockyside can now be described as the hillside on both sides of what is now Route 2 north out of New Cumberland. The land that this section of road was built on was purchased by the West Virginia Department of Highways in 1958[2]. This section of Route 2 was constructed and completed in 1959. This new Route 2 bypassed old Route 66, which was built along the side of the hill overlooking the brickyards. (*This would be the area to the driver's extreme left as you proceed north on Route 2. There are approximately 75 yards separating Route 2 and old Route 66.*)

Below is a view from an old state of West Virginia road map dated 1936 that indicates Route 66 and Route 2 going toward Pughtown, now New Manchester. Shortly after this section of road was completed in 1959, Route 2 replaced Route 66, and Route 8 replaced Route 2.

Photo of map from 1936[3] shows Route 66 and Route 2

Unique to this map are the words "Ferry" next to little arrows. These appear just opposite New Cumberland and then again just under the Route 2 symbol and across from Toronto.

The upper ferry is referring to Black Horse (located just outside of New Cumberland), and the lower ferry is referring to Freeman's Landing. Both of these ferries on the Ohio River played important roles in shipping brick and sewer pipe outside of New Cumberland.

I was fortunate to also obtain the original construction blueprint for this new W.Va. 66 bypass. What is unique about this drawing is the inclusion of a "park area" and "overlook." Unfortunately, the way the road project was designed was not how the project unfolded. There should have been an access road that would have connected old Route 66 to the new Route 2, but for reasons unknown, that didn't take place.

In 2008, under the leadership of George Hines, $20,000 in grant money was obtained from West Virginia Health & Human Resources to build an overlook. Along with financial assistance from the Hancock County Commission, the overlook was completed. A dedication ceremony was held on October 25, 2008, on what is now called Crestview Park. Crestview Park was originally dedicated on October 25, 1963, and over the years walking trails were added to allow the public a majestic view of the Ohio River Valley and a chance to explore this historical site. The overlook completed the project.

23

The following blueprint is a copy that has been traced over to highlight the important characteristics of the construction project. The digital image taken from the original blueprint was faded and indiscernible, so I added highlighting to better define the images on the map so it could be included in this book.

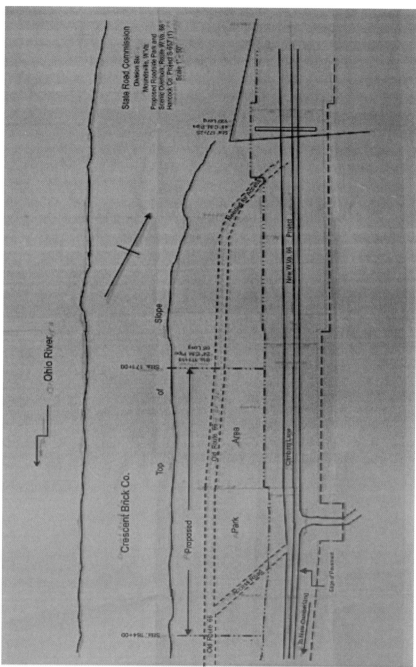

New Route 66 bypass[2] – West Virginia Department of Highways - 1959

Chapter Three
Rockyside a Forgotten Community

The primary focus of this book was to capture the essence of Rockyside, a forgotten mining community, and a place where my parents were born. It became apparent while I was searching for information that very few people knew of or had even heard of Rockyside. Some people associated Rockyside with the road which runs alongside the Rockefeller Center. But most people I spoke with didn't have a clue nor could they visualize an entire community on a hillside that once overlooked the brickyards and the Ohio River.

What makes writing this book difficult is that there seem to be no pictures to show what this community once looked like. We uncovered only a few pictures showing close ups of a brick house, but didn't find one picture that showed the whole community.

Looking at old photos of the brickyards, we could make out where various homes were located along a section of old Route 66. We found nothing that revealed a community where homes, outhouses, water wells, a school, a church, and a barracks once stood.

To make matters worse, we realized that all the buildings, once home to a dozen or more families, had been plowed under and buried when the Route 2 highway cut across the hillside. We soon concluded that probably no pictures were ever taken of this community. An impression of where a church once stood and the broken walls of a school are all that remains. Everything else has disappeared. The hillside is now overgrown with trees and briar bushes, making it difficult even for those people who once actually lived there to remember how it looked so many years ago.

The majority of families who once lived there have all passed away. I was fortunate to have contacted a few of their children about writing this book. When I mentioned

Rockyside, they seemed surprised. To some, hearing the word Rockyside brought back a flood of memories, and many said they had forgotten all about it. Some remembered how hard the conditions were living on the hillside, so far from town, tending to cows and chickens before and after school, or working a vegetable garden in hard rocky soil, or making bread for the men in the barracks. Some remembered walking over a mile to the Catholic school in town.

Now, looking at this hillside, nothing remotely resembles the small community where nearly 12 homes, a church, and school once stood. This small mining community that was originally the home for some 200 men working the brickyards and clay mines later became the home for an additional 90 men, women, and children. It stood for nearly 40 years but now no longer exists. However, the people who helped us with this book did remember living, playing, going to school, and even attending church on this hillside. For these people, Rockyside still exists, if just in their memory. For others, Rockyside never existed at all.

Mostly men, who came from Eastern Europe, populated this rough rocky hillside area and were identified as Poles and Slavs. These men came from Poland, Austria, Czechoslovakia, Russia, and Germany. Both sets of my grandparents came to the United States from either Poland or Austria.

At the end of this section is a computer drawing of Rockyside put together from numerous conversations with people who still remember what the hillside once looked like. The drawing of course is not to scale but does reflect where this entire small community of mining and brickmaking families once lived. The drawing was the result of numerous conversations with Mr. John Kuzio, cousin Gertrude Ludovici, Helen Brancazio, and Mr. Ed Reese. These people remembered certain but oftentimes different aspects of this hillside. It was funny how each remembered something differently. What I am representing is a collective, best effort drawing, indicating what families lived there, and where their homes were located.

Families living on this hillside around 1900 to 1940 were, as best evidence could provide: Angus, Narkevich, Spilecki, Czernecki, Stolarczyk, Turoff, Sweat, Zielinsky, Zucosky, Salisberry, McNickols, Zubrycki, two Reese families, Zumer, and Bagienski. Of course, the spelling of their last

28

names changed over time as well. These families raised their children on Rockyside until sometime in the mid to late 1940's when they gradually moved into the nearby town of New Cumberland.

In the early days, around 1844, when ground breaking for the first brickyards started, the hillside was quite barren. There were no homes at that time. A single large building that became known as "the barracks" was erected around 1850. Later, a second building would be built alongside this building and would be used for a dining facility.

This barracks building was erected close to the existing Rockyside Road, or where the state police building is currently located. It was made from wood and wood timbers since brickmaking was just getting started. The barracks stood until around 1920 when it was completely destroyed by fire. It was later rebuilt, but higher on the hillside, in the vicinity of the first Catholic Church. This new building was built from brick. *Searching for remnants of this building were unsuccessful despite numerous trips looking at varying locations. No evidence of where this building was built could be found. The only explanation is the building was closer to where the highway (Route 2) now runs and was plowed under when the road was constructed.*

The barracks housed only single men, of which there were upwards of 200 during peak periods. Some of these men couldn't take the struggles and hardships of working in either the brickyards or the adjoining mines. Some would work for a short time and then move on trying to find work elsewhere.

There were actually two buildings built; the barracks was used for sleeping, and a second somewhat smaller building was used as a place for the men to take their meals. The young girls living on the hillside would help prepare bread and other items for the men's meals. Some would also help clean and make beds. Most girls working in the barracks, typically before or sometimes after school, often found their future husbands in the mix. Ironically, some single men were actually taken in as boarders into the nearby homes to help contribute to that house's wellbeing. The Zumer home was one such home, according to my mother.

The early years of brick making started with the Aetna (Etna), Cunningham, and the Clifton kilns all situated along the edge of the river. These three brickyards attracted most of the workers from within the town of New Cumberland. Others were brought over from Europe by Captain John Porter himself. It wasn't until the late 1870's when the Union, Eagle, and Rockyside brickyards were established that the hillside began to grow in population. The clay mines which supplied the necessary materials were all situated near these brickyards.

The brickyards, including Crescent and Globe, were all individually operated. It remained that way until 1894 when the Mack Manufacturing Company purchased all the brickyards and clay mines with the exception of Globe. They were able to consolidate and run all these facilities like a true business venture. One set of journals provided the names of those working at the individual plants or mines, how much they worked and were paid, what they were charged for room and board, and any store items they purchased on credit. This process continued until the companies were either closed or later, like Crescent and Union, were sold. Crescent and a portion of Union kept operating well into the late 1970's. The last Crescent mine, located on Hardins Run Road, was closed in 1979, and brickmaking concluded in early 1980.

Some of the single men working in this area would eventually meet up with their future wives here. As more men were married, the Mack Company decided to build homes and provide more suitable housing. These homes were all built along the hillside, close to the brickyards. The community really started to become populated by the late 1890's and early 1900's.

The houses built for the workers were made entirely out of brick and were constructed in the pattern of two duplex homes. Each side consisted of four rooms; two on the top floor and two on the bottom floor, with fireplaces on both floors. Restroom facilities were not part of the house. Outhouses were constructed separately and placed slightly away from the homes. The outdoor privies provided adequate room for a number of people at one time. Also, "spring houses" were constructed for drinking water. A number of these were located along the hillside. One spring house was very close to a clay tipple for the Union brickyard and close to the Zumer house. Families would use buckets to carry water back to their homes to help prepare meals or wash clothes.

The first Catholic Church, Immaculate Conception, was built on this hillside overlooking the Ohio River in 1904. The physical location was directly behind the Union Brickyard about 100-yards off of Route 66. It was dug back into the hillside using large pieces of sewer pipe with bricks inserted into the sewer pipe as a foundation. This wooden structure was erected quickly, taking less than four months to complete, and was dedicated Christmas Eve 1904. The steeple to the church didn't get put on until spring. The church steeple had a small brass bell that would ring to let people in the area know it was time for church services to begin.

Less than 50 yards north of the church was a one-room schoolhouse, Rockyside School. This school, constructed entirely from brick, had at least three teachers and remained open until around 1938. Remnants of the brick structure are still visible today. Schoolteachers were Ms. Alice Cooper[1], Mr. Tony LaNeve[2], and Ms. Eleanor Burskey[3].

There were, as best information reveals, approximately six large brick duplex homes with two families occupying each home. There was one large clapboard house, duplex of sorts, with seven rooms on one side and five rooms on the other. There were four smaller wooden homes that each had four to five smaller rooms. Each of these houses was occupied by one family, and several had a large porch, as did the Zumer home.

All of these homes were arranged the same. The living and sleeping quarters were located on the top floor. The kitchen and ground storage were located on the bottom. This allowed any meats, cheeses, and milk products to be slightly below ground to take advantage of the coolness the ground provided.

Each family had a small piece of ground they used for growing vegetables on top of the hillside. Some families had cows and chickens which provided milk and eggs. Many families made their own cheeses. Families shared what they had with their neighbors, and all kept a watchful eye on each other.

Families started to move away from Rockyside between 1930 and mid-1940's to relocate into the town of New Cumberland. By early 1950, all families had vacated the hillside.

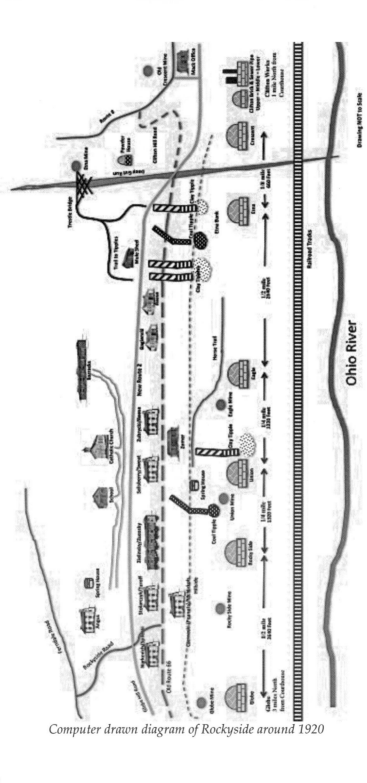

Computer drawn diagram of Rockyside around 1920

Chapter Four
Clay Mining in Hancock County, WV

Clay mining was first started near the mouth of Holberts Run in 1830 when Mr. John Gamble began taking clay and shipping it to Pittsburgh, PA. He mined and sent the clay that would be used to make bricks for the steel mills in Pittsburgh.

In 1832, the first brickyard was established at a site called W. B. Freeman Brickworks. Mr. W. B. Freeman and Mr. James S. Porter partnered the idea of making the brick at the actual source of the clay and opened the first of many brickyards in the area. They decided to profit by making the actual bricks that the clay was being used for in Pittsburgh. In the early days, they supplied roughly 200,000[1] bricks annually to the steel and iron works in Pittsburgh.

So, what actually is clay? Clay[2] is a soft, loose, earthy material made up of a number of minerals rich in alumina, silica, and water. Clay can also be stiff, and yellow, red, or bluish-gray in color. Clay is formed from the weathering and erosion of rocks from the mineral group feldspar (known as the "mother of clay") and is made of particles with a grain size of less than four micrometers over vast periods of time. Clay is common and can be found all over the world. When wet, most clay can be molded and formed into shapes. When exposed to very high temperatures, clay can become as hard as stone. This is why clay is used to make various items such as bricks, sewer pipe, and pottery.

Clay was used first and foremost to make bricks in Hancock County, and most clay mines were located very close to actual brickyards. This was evident with the first brickyard at W. B. Freeman about one mile south of New Cumberland.

As brickyards sprang up, both north and south of New Cumberland, the clay mines had to be discovered first. Each brickyard had its own mine, and these mines were located as close to the brick operation as possible. As mines dried up, either new veins were discovered, or an entirely new mine needed to be found. This was the case with the Crescent mines. The first mine was located near the intersection of what is now Route 2 and Route 8, along the hillside driving north up Route 8. The second mine was located just south along North Chestnut Street, off of what was called Chestnut Alley. Finally, the last Crescent mine was found a short distance away on Hardins Run Road.

These mines were all found using the old-fashioned digging method to find the clay. Sometimes dynamite would be used to open up enough area to determine if further digging was worthwhile. In order to find clay, miners needed to know the correct rock progression. It started by first finding sandstone, then shale, coal, and finally clay. This progression holds true for all clay discoveries. In some cases, the coal wasn't removed because it was too soft (bituminous), which really wasn't good for producing high temperatures required to bake brick. Most generally, a means was found to go directly into the veins of clay leaving the coal and sandstone intact.

Once a clay vein was exposed, a process was needed to break up the clay so it could be removed. Once broken up, clay[3] would be loaded into clay cars that rested on narrow railroad tracks. These cars then left the mine by gravity and were pulled back into the mines by either mules, known as "mule power" or horses. In 1912, mechanized equipment became available to aid the miners' digging and removal efforts.

The mines in Hancock County are called "self draining;" this is to say, no pumps are used, and water will flow from the mines in a small stream into the river. This is still evident today in many locations both north and south of New Cumberland. It is interesting to note that the mines located on the Ohio side of the river are sloped in the opposite direction, so pumps have to be used to exhaust the water.

The Mack Manufacturing Company[3] had the most simplistic system. Manual labor was used to strip away the sandstone, shale, and other rock formations, and after the opening into the hill measured roughly 12 feet, a crib was built of heavy timber. This crib opening would become the actual

34

mine entrance. Debris between the timbers would be added for additional support to the overall structure. Since only a small portion of the shale was used in the brickmaking operation, it was often used to wedge between the timbers.

Picture of the Crescent Mine with Crib installed around entrance
Photo courtesy of Mack Manufacturing Company

Diggers were obliged to go as far back into the hillside as they could in order to find all of the clay veins. Some veins measured 15 to 25 feet in thickness.

A device known as a "jumper"[4] and a heavy sledge were sometimes employed. Two men worked on a crew; one would hold the "jumper" while the other wielded the sledge. At other times, a bore and drill were used, but this required much effort by both miners. Miners would start to blast as soon as they struck a vein, using dynamite and ordinary blasting powder.

Holes were bored every five feet, and then the clay was "shot." Dynamite sticks were dropped into these holes, and the holes were angled so that when the explosion occurred, the clay was fractured enough to be removed in large pieces.

Charges placed too close together resulted in the clay breaking up into fine pieces, making it harder to extract because it now had other minerals and material mixed in with the clay.

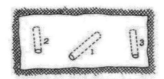

Shows different shot methods of drilling into the Clay. Charges would go off in sequence to get the maximum breakup

Dynamite was stored away from the mining and brickmaking operation for safety purposes. That was also the case at the Mack mines. A circular building was constructed out of three alternating brick rows, log cabin style, and finished with a brick and concrete roof. To complete the building, a heavy metal door was hung to protect the dynamite and blasting powders from the elements. This building was known as a "powder house." We were very fortunate to find this powder house still standing, located a couple hundred yards up into Deep Gut Run.

Powder House used by miners to store dynamite and blasting powder
Photo courtesy of T. W. Zielinsky

All the clay was dug entirely by hand. A typical crew consisting of two men would mine an average of 20 tons of clay per day. The workers loaded the clay into "clay cars" or "carts." Sometime the clay cars, once out of the mine, needed pulled toward the tipples, and mules were used to perform this task. Once the cars reached the tipple, they were tipped over, allowing the clay to fall to the ground in piles. The clay was then weathered for four weeks or so. Then miners would move the clay into a large building, called a clay processing building, equipped with "rolls"[3] or "clappers."[3] These devices rolled or clapped the clay, breaking down the large chunks to a powdery form. After achieving the correct fineness, the clay was then taken to a "wet pan"[3] or "pugmill"[3] where water was mixed with the clay to produce a batter-like consistency. The consistency was similar to that of stiff mud. Next the clay was moved to auger machines that formed the clay into bricks. The bricks were either allowed to dry in the sun or placed on drying beds. After drying, the bricks were taken to the kilns where they were readied for firing. The fire was kindled inside a beehive styled kiln where the roof of the kiln was covered with ashes to hold the heat inside. These were known as beehive "downdraft"[3] kilns.

Most mines had single gravity tracks installed, much like those in the first Etna Mine. Cars coming out of the second Etna Mine, located across Deep Gut, came out by gravity but required mules to pull them around the hill and up to the tipples.

Clay is formed under a layer of coal. On top of the coal sits a layer of sandstone rock called a "roll." Once a roll was hit, the clay was exhausted, and workers then had to find new clay veins. Once the Crescent Mine came in contact with a "roll," workers drilled for almost a year, through nearly 530 feet of stone before striking a new clay vein. Another "roll" was found in the Union Mine nearly 1300 feet long, and a "roll" in the Rockyside Mine nearly 1600 feet in length. Clay miners have stated that this run of sandstone extends all along the West Virginia hill facing the Ohio River, and that sooner or later all clay mines will run against the "roll."[5]

The clay in Hancock County is called fire clay. These very high quality clays have flint-like properties that allow them to sustain high temperatures after being made into brick. This type of clay exists in all the mines in this area. It is of medium-hard consistency, gray in color, and typically mixed with some shale prior to entering the brick machine. The clay is known as either Kittanning or Clarion Fire Clay.

These main clay veins or seams vary, but on average are relatively the same. Etna and Crescent Mines have a vein slope of 1 inch to over 16 feet; in the Rockyside Mine the slope is 2 inches to 16 feet, and in the Union Mine the slope is 3 inches to 16 feet, which is quite substantial.

This clay seam, as measured vertically from the floor of the Ohio River, measures some 750 feet above sea level and stays at about that same height from Clifton north all the way to Globe.[5] Ironically, nearly the same height can be measured from east of Etna all the way south to the mouth of Kings Creek before it tapers slightly to 650 feet above sea level. This means the dip in the clay seam is 100 feet in four miles or 25 feet to one mile, and then the clay passes under the Ohio River three-fourths of a mile below the mouth of Kings Creek.[6]

These clay mines were often abandoned after a "roll" was discovered and additional penetration was done to prove the clay seam had expired. Such is the case from Globe, Rockyside, and Union mines. Union and its various seams were considered the largest of all the mines in that area. From the mine map provided to the writers, it truly can be classified as the largest clay mine in the area.

Something unique was discovered while researching the Etna Clay Mine. All clay mine entrances were essentially next to the brickyards they served, which were along the bottom of the hillside near the Ohio River. These clay seams were then mined from the bottom to the top of the hill. This followed the natural contour of the clay and allowed gravity tracks to bring the clay cars out of the mine. The Etna mines were discovered on both the left and right side of Deep Gut Run going north up Etna Hollow. The larger entrance appears to be situated across the ravine on the right side. This mine was dug under what is now Route 8 angled toward New Cumberland. The other entrance was located high on the left side of the hill facing the river and has been completely sealed.

A large trestle bridge was built across Deep Gut Run bridging the hillsides. Clay was mined deep into the hillside under Route 8 with shafts that led to parts of the first Crescent Clay Mine.

Trestle Bridge for Etna Mine
Rare photo courtesy of George Hines

Clay was removed from this mine in cars, with gravity allowing the cars to cross the bridge. Mules then pulled the cars around and along the left side of the hill, (see the wooden support rails), and then up to the tipples. Narrow railroad tracks were installed to take the clay cars to the tipple for dumping.

The above photo doesn't reflect what this area actually looks like today. Over one hundred years of water runoff and earth shifting have eroded the gulley and the land on either side. The bank to the mine, on the right side, is extremely steep with no sign of the bridge. We did find the entrance to the Etna Mine, but it is entirely filled with several feet of water and totally impassable. On the left side of the hill, railroad tracks are still lying on rotten timbers and are the only sign left of the mining effort.

The exception to these clay mines is the Union Mine. This mine was the largest of all mines in this area and was located outside on the hillside very close to the clay processing building. This mine was so large that it required two gravity tracks to bring cars out from the main entrance. Inside the mine, multiple tracks were also used to get the clay to the entrance. The tracks coming out were curved, using the side of the horse trail as a natural banking process to ascend to the tipple. These cars were then pulled up by a cable system and then tipped, allowing the clay to fall through an open vertical shaft. This vertical shaft was connected to a chute angled under the railroad tracks and positioned directly into the clay processing building. The Union clay building is still standing and is very much intact. This is the only and last remaining building of the entire brickyard. The railroad track (in photo, bottom left) hugs the hillside and extends all the way to the Rockyside brickyard.

The photo below is the Union incline leading to the tipple. Cars (white circles) are positioned on both tracks, and they alternate. As one car goes up to get dumped, the other gets hooked to the cable, then the process repeats for the other car.

Photo of Union Mine incline – cars would come out from below the railroad track seen to the left – Photo courtesy of Mack Manufacturing Company

This next photo is an aerial of the Union clay processing building that is still standing. The photo shows where the clay actually entered into the top of the building for processing. The front of the building is where the bricks were made. To the right side of the building was a drying building (now removed) where bricks were dried prior to being moved to the kilns for firing.

Photo of Union clay processing building – clay entry point was near hillside
Photo courtesy of Google Maps

Stories from Alex Zucosky (deceased) and Helen Brancazio stated that the "boys," on days when the mine wasn't operating, would push cars back as far as they could into the mine, jump in the car, and ride them out and up the incline. One Sunday morning almost proved fatal. On one ride the car came out so fast it proceeded to the top of the incline and nearly tipped over. Fortunately, a workman at the top, seeing the oncoming car, placed a large board across the tracks that stopped the car short of the tipping point. *No more Sunday rides for them.*

Chemical analyses of clays taken from the Crescent and Etna mines show Lower Kittanning coal resting on six feet of bluish-gray flint fire clay, and below this was four feet of the gray shale clay with ten to twelve feet of blue shale clay under the gray. In the manufacturing of bricks, the three varieties are often mixed.[7]

Clarion clay, which is also in abundance in this area, is especially adapted to the manufacturing of sewer pipe. The clay was sampled at an entry point at the Etna plant and was determined to be better suited for sewer pipe than brickmaking. This clay was also found in the Crescent Mine across from the Clifton Works and used specifically by Clifton in the making of sewer pipe.

All the mines in this northern section were very similar in mineral makeup. As an example of the Rockyside mine:[8]

Rock layers (strata) for the Rockyside Mine

	Ft.	In.
Sandstone	40	0
Coal Kittanning	2½	0
Flint Clay	6	0
Gray Shale Clay	4	0
Blue Shale Clay	12	0
Sandstone Floor	4	0
Fine Laminated Shale	40	0
Coal Clarion	0	3
Clay Clarion	10	0

Based on the above data, clay for the most part is found primarily near the river bottom and is worked upward toward the sandstone to take advantage of the natural contour of the rock progression.

This type of Clarion clay has high water content, so it is used exclusively for making sewer pipe. In the manufacturing of bricks and paving bricks, the flint clay and the gray and blue shales are mixed together.

As of 1923, there were approximately 30 different mines extending from the northern part of Hancock County to the bends following Kings Creek. There were approximately another 30 mines from Kings Creek south past Wellsburg, WV.[9]

Anyone traveling north on Route 2 coming into New Cumberland will notice large sandstone formations along this stretch of road. A vein of coal is visible directly under the sandstone that reaches just to the top of the roadway. Directly under this coal is a vein of clay. It was this coal and clay that supplied those very first brickyards.

Chapter Five
Brickmaking South of New Cumberland

The south end of New Cumberland is where brickmaking and brickyards first started. After Mr. John Gamble discovered the flint fire clay on his property near the mouth of Holberts Run in 1830, he and Mr. Thomas Freeman decided to build a brickyard. Their reasoning was that it would be easier to make the bricks at the source of the clay instead of hauling the clay to Pittsburgh and then having someone else make the bricks.

In the spring of 1832, Mr. James S. Porter along with Mr. W. B. Freeman started the very first brickyard near the mouth of Holberts Run, naming it the W. B. Freeman Brickyard. Then about two years later, Mr. Thomas Freeman followed his family and began building a little farther south. This area became known as Freeman's Landing. Not only were bricks made here, but since the landing was located on the Ohio River, a ferry service was also developed. The ferry was a convenient place to conduct business for both brick workers and farmers in the vicinity and served as a home market for transporting their products.

Around this same time, Mr. Thomas Freeman, Mr. Mahan, and Mr. James Porter started a brickyard in 1834 known as the Claymont Plant of the Porter Brick Company. These men continued to scout this area, and in 1837 partnered with Mr. Phillip Beall to begin a new business under Porter & Beall. They started their first brickyard north of the mouth of Kings Creek. This became known as the Lone Star Brick Works.

In that same year, Porter & Beall also began building a brickyard just north of Lone Star called the Sligo Brickyard. This area was just south of Zalia and owned by the Standish Brick Company from Toronto, OH.[1]

Also in 1837, Mr. Thomas Anderson started his brickyard just north of the Sligo location and named it the

Anderson Brickyard. This plant would eventually make sewer pipe and was finally converted to a clay manufacturing plant before it closed.

In 1844, Mr. James and William Porter began a brickyard just a quarter mile south of the New Cumberland city limits known as Mahan, Porter, & Company Brickyard. The name would eventually be changed to the Black-Horse Works because the plant sat next to the famous Black Horse tavern. It was around this time that all the plant owners began to claim land north of New Cumberland. It seemed that 1844 was a turning point when the majority of new yards were started in the northern part of town. These yards included the Aetna (Etna), Cunningham, and the Clifton Fire Brick plants.

Freeman's Landing W. B. Freeman Plant
The First Brickyard Plant

Brickmaking started one mile south of New Cumberland at a point known as W. B. Freeman Brickyard. There are few pictures of this area with the exception of this Freeman's Landing picture. Other brickyards in this area were never photographed. There are, however, diagrams of the individual plants as developed by the Sanborn Fire Insurance Company, and these are placed in the Photo Section of this book.

Freeman's Landing South of New Cumberland
Picture courtesy of West Virginia Film Office

44

Freeman's Landing, the first brickyard of W. B. Freeman, began operating in 1832 with one Corliss engine. The capacity of the drying yard was nearly 40,000 bricks. A Martin brick machine was used to shape the bricks, and the plant incorporated four kilns for burning the bricks. Since coal was of great abundance, a mixture of coal and wood was used to heat the kilns.[1]   In later years, the upper building would be used for crushing clay in a Blake Crusher, having a capacity of nearly 100 tons a day.

This plant also included a small Raymond auger machine with a capacity of marking 25,000 bricks, and the machine used several dies for both bricks and tiles of various special designs. Whether the bricks were molded by hand or on the special auger machine, they were dried on the large floor inside the building by using steam. This plant remained open until around 1942.

Lone Star Brick Works

The Lone Star Brick Works was started in 1837 but remained idle until 1845 when it went into production. It was located roughly two and one-half miles south of New Cumberland at the mouth of Kings Creek. This plant was small when initially built and consisted of a small auger machine, a nine-foot dry pan, a twelve-arch drying floor, and five downdraft kilns. This plant remained open for only a couple of years before it closed. It is believed the lack of available clay for this plant created financial hardships that moved it to close sooner than anticipated.

Sligo Brick and Sewer Pipe Plant

This plant was also started 1837 around the same time as the Lone Star plant. It was located just north of Lone Star, about two miles south of New Cumberland. Equipment at the plant included a wet pan, three drying floors, and a Means press with a 40-inch steam cylinder and an 18-inch clay cylinder. The yard also had eleven downdraft kilns. The Standish Brick Company from Toronto, Ohio, owned the plant property while Porter and Beall Company made the financial investment.

This plant started as a brickmaking facility and was converted to sewer pipe around 1890 before it closed in 1902. The plant stayed in operational condition until around 1910 when it was decided it would no longer make sewer pipe and was torn down.

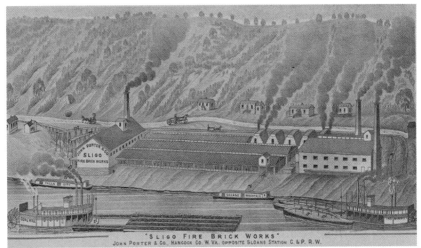

Artist rendering of Sligo Plant from 1837 first plant built north of the mouth of Kings Creek – Drawing courtesy of History of Brickmaking page 219

Actual picture of the Sligo Plant before shutting down in 1904
Photo courtesy of Mack Manufacturing

Anderson Brothers Brickyard & Sewer Pipe

This plant was also started in 1837 about one and three-quarter miles south of New Cumberland, just north of the Sligo plant. Little information was available for this plant. It was a relatively small plant with a moulding and drying building and a steam-drying house. It consisted of 8 downdraft kilns and was unique in that it had direct access to clay from the hills along the southern part of what is now Route 2.

By 1897 the plant changed ownership and became McElfresh Clay Company, but closed by early 1900. In its last few years, the plant only crushed clay for outbound shipments.

Claymont Brick and Tile Brick Works

The Claymont Plant was the second plant started by the Porter Company in 1834 and was located one and a half miles south of New Cumberland. This plant was built in two sections; the lower section was equipped with a nine-foot drying pan, a pug mill, and Bucyrus auger machine with a capacity of 30,000 bricks. They were burned in eleven round downdraft kilns, 26 and 28 feet in diameter, holding 50,000 to 60,000 bricks each.

The upper building section was part of the original Freeman plant, so these plants were very close together. It contained a Raymond auger, a Blake crusher, and large drying floors that used steam for drying.

This plant changed ownership by 1897 to T. J. Garlick & Company, and then by 1902 it was changed again and became known again as the Claymont Brick and Tile Works.

N. W. Ballantyne Clay Grinding

The Ballantyne Clay Grinding plant was located near the bottom of Ballantyne Hill Road three-quarters mile south of New Cumberland. It supplied clay to most of the brickyards south of this location. It was purchased and rebuilt in early

1896 and became known as the West Virginia Fire Clay Company and Clay Grinding. The plant produced refined clay for outbound shipments to Pittsburgh and Wheeling.

In this plant, equipment consisted of a Blake crusher with two nine-foot drying pans, each with a capacity of 200 tons of crushed clay per day. All the clay was taken from the hillside directly above the plant. The vein of clay in this location was flint fire clay, roughly six and one-half feet thick with a coal seam directly above the clay nearly three feet thick. These two seams ran nearly 800 feet south until hitting a sandstone roll, cutting off both the coal and clay.

This plant remained operational until 1948 when it underwent a re-modernization and continued mining clay from two strip mines and one drift mine. This plant closed its mining operations in 1963.

Black-Horse Brick and Sewer Pipe

The Black-Horse plant was started in 1844 just one-quarter mile south of New Cumberland. It was originally named Mahan, Porter, & Company Sewer Pipe and Fire Brick. It was situated near the old Black Horse tavern and ferry just outside of town limits. Shortly after the plant began, the name was changed to the Black-Horse Works. The American Sewer Pipe Company purchased the plant in 1910 and again changed the name to reflect the new owners.

Brick and sewer pipe were both initially produced. Sewer pipe was made until 1896; then the plant was converted back to bricks. In 1923, American Vitrified purchased the assets and continued to make bricks until that plant closed as well.

During its years of operation, this plant molded bricks in a Freese auger machine, which had a daily capacity of 60,000 building bricks or 40,000 paving bricks. The bricks were repressed on two double mold Raymond and two double mold Richardson machines. The plant had two drying tunnels, and the clay was mined directly from the plant through a 2,300-foot long entry.

These companies were the brick and sewer pipe plants south of New Cumberland. I've included another computer drawing of where these plants were located in relation to New Cumberland. You can also see where the Chelsea China Company was located, as well as the People's store and Cutler Steel/Duraloy Company. Several apartment buildings and company houses were located just north of the Duraloy Company. I've listed those families living in the homes around 1920, including John Kuzio's family.

Families that lived just south of the Mack Office lived in either an apartment building or in one of the small homes built by the Mack Company. Some of the families living here when John Kuzio was born are as follows: Biela, Hoder, Kuzio, Burskey, Zimlas, and Clark. The Clark family was one of only a few black families living in New Cumberland at that time. There were several black families when I was growing up, but all had moved away by early 1960.

Not all of the brickyards that were once located near New Cumberland are reflected on this drawing. These yards sprang up practically overnight, were operated for a few years, and then sold to new owners. Plants like the Lone Star Brickyard were built and then abandoned a short time later. Despite being smaller in size, these brickyards south of New Cumberland did produce high quality bricks. Clay seams were found all along the ridge of the hillside outside of New Cumberland clear to the mouth of Kings Creek.

One amazing fact is that in 1837, bricks were being made at about 200,000 bricks per year from these southern brickyards. These bricks primarily traveled to Pittsburgh to be used in the iron works, while other bricks made their way to Wheeling, and Cincinnati, Ohio. By 1844, with the iron trade increasing, brick production had grown to over 500,000 bricks annually to supply the Pittsburgh iron market alone.

In 1844, total brick production grew to more than 1,500,000 annually. Production in 1867 reached 7,800,000 bricks. By 1873 production reached a peak of 11,000,000 bricks and 12,000 tons of fire clay annually. [2]

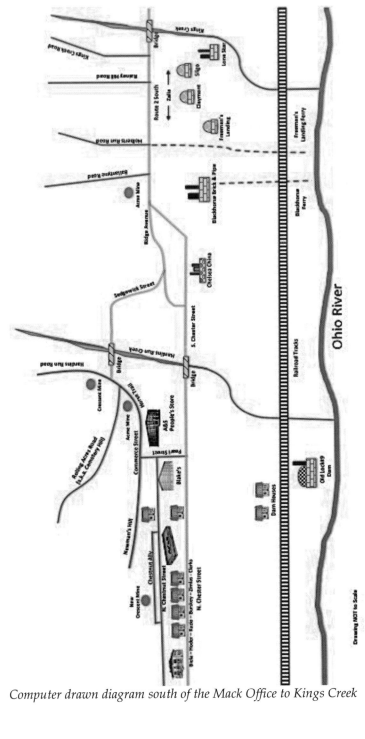

Computer drawn diagram south of the Mack Office to Kings Creek

Chapter Six
Brickmaking North of New Cumberland

Brickmaking in early 1830 was a far cry from how bricks are manufactured today. This part of the Ohio River was often referred to as "brickyard bend" because of the bend in the river and because Hancock County and New Cumberland were known as the largest clay and brick center in West Virginia. The primary reason for this is that Hancock County is rich in Clarion and Lower Kittanning clays which are used in the manufacture of building and paving brick, with Clarion clays used mainly for making sewer pipe. The shale that is found between these two clays was used to manufacture common brick. Anyone growing up in New Cumberland is part of this fabulous history.

So it began. Over a distance of seven miles stretched an area that was so important in the manufacture of bricks and sewer pipe that it staggers the imagination. Our first picture captures the Clifton (Lower) Works for sewer pipe production.

The Clifton Works consisted of three separate plants; Clifton Upper, Middle, and Lower. The lower works primarily made sewer pipe. The date the picture was taken is unknown. Thousands of pieces of pipe and tile can be seen, with even more extending farther north and south. They were sorted by size and shape and stacked in neat rows.

Sewer Pipe storage yard of the Clifton Works just south of the Mack Office shown in center – In the upper right corner is a tipple to the first Crescent clay mine, which would be located today at the intersection of Routes 2&8

Manufacturing concerns in these early brick-making plants were very minor. A typical crew of four or five men could successfully operate an entire plant. Because clay had to dry in the sun before the production process started, the early manufacturing of bricks had to take place in the summer. During the winter months, the same crew of workers often went into the clay mines and dug the necessary amount of clay for the upcoming summer months. The process of mining was extremely difficult and required great strength from the miners.

Although the hills surrounding the plants had plenty of coal, only wood was used in the early days as fire for the bricks. There was a general belief that only wood had the correct temperature to bake the bricks correctly. After the bricks were fired for a sufficient time, they were removed from the kilns. As the bricks were removed, workers always found soft bricks on the top of the pile, burned and warped bricks on the bottom of the pile, and good bricks in the middle. In the spring when the rains came and the melting snow had raised the river level, the bricks were loaded by hand onto riverboats and sent to market.

Brickmaking continue to evolve, and with each new brickyard, newer ways of making the job easier were discovered. In 1862, a stock company looking for oil sunk a well high up in Deep Gut Run north of New Cumberland on land owned by Mr. Joseph Stuart. They failed to strike oil, but did strike a supply of gas, which for volume and pureness has never been equaled in the world. Not knowing the value of this gas, and not obtaining any oil, the company abandoned their lease, and for years this fountain of gas was allowed to just "roar." The deafening noise lasted for almost two years until the well was accidentally ignited. Flames were said to have shot eighty feet in the air, lighting up this section of Deep Gut for miles around.

People from all over the county came to view this sight as the well blazed for more than a year. Many tries at smothering the flame were met with disappointment. Great stones and dirt were thrown on the flame, as well as old carpets soaked in water, but still the fire and flame raged on. Then as simply as the flame was turned on, it was turned off. A couple of people noticed that the stones near the mouth of the flame were red hot from the heat. They stood on opposite sides of the flame, and at the same time threw their buckets of water upon the heated stones. A "hiss" – a sudden spread of steam cut the flame, and the fire was out.

The land was then leased to a Philadelphia company for the purpose of producing carbon or "soot." A soot factory operated for years and was managed by Mr. Billy Hooper, Steenrod Bambrick, Jake Wilson, and Dan McDonald. Printer's ink was made from the soot and was used in the publishing of Harper's Magazine and Godey's Ladies' Book. The product was even exported to Europe before the soot factory was destroyed by fire in 1886.[2]

However, ten years earlier, while the gas was still flowing, a large pipe was laid between the gas well and the Clifton plant. This was the first plant to actually use gas to run two Corliss engines and bake all the bricks that were made in these two yards.

During the same year, another well was sunk close to the first, at a depth of about 600 feet. This produced another well, equal in output to that of the first well. This was the beginning of using gas as a heating source for the kilns and brickyards at the north end of New Cumberland.

It is also important to note that even with brickmaking in the United States just beginning, foreign competition was already seeping into the market. The problem became so great that in 1843, a short 13 years after brickmaking started in this area, Congress needed to step in. Congress, in answer to a petition for an increase in tariff rates upon foreign brick, granted further protection to the home brick industry. This allowed the American workmen to establish pricing that was satisfactory to both the producer and the consumer. The foreign bricks came mostly from England and cost an exorbitant amount, $100 and even $125 per thousand. The established tariffs allowed the price to drop dramatically so competition could resume to normal.[1]

A Brief Overview of the Mack Operations

A description of each plant will follow this overview of the Mack Manufacturing Company. Mack consolidated the operations of the Rockyside, Union, Eagle, Etna, Crescent, Clifton, and Sligo plants in 1894. Once Sligo closed, Mack concentrated on the remaining plants north of New Cumberland.

As mentioned earlier, clay was removed from mines close to the brickmaking operations. Dry pans were used at each operation to dry the clay prior to sending it to a pugmill. Pugmills were used to mix the clay with water and sometimes shale to achieve the necessary consistency before moving the clay to a brick making auger machine. Bonnot or Stevenson auger machines were used to make the bricks, each having a capacity of 50,000 bricks per day.

Bricks leaving an auger machine were called "green bricks." The "green bricks" were taken from the machines on double-decker cars and moved on the various railroad tracks to the drying beds. These drying beds were made of bricks and were about 100 feet long by 45 feet wide. The drier contained 10 tunnels that would hold some 70 cars. A firebox furnace at each tunnel provided the hot-air drying necessary to dry the bricks. Typically, 18 to 24 hours was needed before moving the bricks to the kilns.

In total, there were roughly 80 or so kilns that resembled large beehives. These round beehive-shaped kilns were the downdraft type, with large iron bands around the circumference and turn buckles at the large metal doors. Each kiln averaged 28 to 30 feet in diameter and had a bottom flue, opening into a stack (chimney) about 45 feet high. Typically, two kilns used one stack, but it wasn't uncommon for three or four kilns to use the same stack.

The type of power equipment that was used also varied as described below, but all plants used Corliss engines. These plants used a total of 13 horizontal single expansion engines with a range from 250 to 400 horsepower. Six smaller engines were used for smaller purposes. These Corliss engines were steam driven, using a total of 24 tubular boilers to supply the steam for the engines.

Mack produced three types of brick; wire-cut, repressed, and Mack block of a special shape used for paving against the streetcar rails and railway tracks. The company manufactured building bricks, paving bricks, sewer pipe of all sizes, flue linings, furnace bricks, and made specialty-furnishing bricks for specific work. The Mack brickyards didn't work twelve months a year. The brickyards produced brick for nine to eleven months and used the non-productive months to clean up and repair the kilns and facilities. The brickyards alternated so brick production was constant while one or more yards were shut down for maintenance and repair. The workforce averaged 300 workers across all of the Mack facilities. A review of actual payroll journals indicated between 1901 through 1914 the number of workers averaged roughly 400 workers. This larger number included both brickmaking and clay mining operations.

To begin working our way north out of New Cumberland, I first must touch on the Acme Clay Works. This facility was actually built inside the city limits of New Cumberland, so here we must start.

Acme Clay Works

Alfred H. Chapman started and operated the Chapman Foundry in 1851. Known for the production of both clay and coal, the plant was located at the intersection of Commerce and Straight Streets and directly opposite from what is now New Cumberland City Park.

In 1901, the foundry was converted to an all clay production plant, grinding flint fire clay for shipment, and was renamed the Acme Clay Works. The plant was equipped with two drying pans and had a daily production of over 100 tons of clay. It is unknown when the plant was closed; however, the smoke stack (chimney) and other partial buildings still remain.

The foundry and all associated equipment was moved into New Cumberland at the site of the Hancock County Manufacturing building at Taylor and South Chester Streets.

Photo of the Acme Clay Works during high water – taken from the present site of the New Cumberland City Park on February 15, 1948
Photo courtesy of the Hancock County Courier

Clifton Fire Brick Company

The Clifton Fire Brick Works that eventually became a sewer pipe company was the most difficult plant to research. Starting in 1844 as the Clifton Fire Brick Company, it was sold just a year later in 1845, changing hands again in 1846. Over the years, there were three different plants.

The first Clifton plant was built as the Lower Works, and then later the Middle and Upper Clifton Works were added. The Crescent Plant bordered the Upper Clifton Works, and the two merged in 1871 when the Crescent Brickyard took over the Upper Works.

The plant first started making bricks but soon converted to making sewer pipe. Plant equipment consisted of a large wet pan, three drying floors, a Means press with a 40-inch steam cylinder and an 18-inch clay cylinder. The sewer pipe was burned in twelve downdraft kilns which were either 28 or 30 feet in diameter.

The Mack Manufacturing Company consolidated the Clifton Works along with several other plants in 1894. Up to the point when the plant was idled in 1902, it was considered the premier sewer pipe manufacturer.

Crescent Brick Plant

The Crescent Brick Plant was started a couple of hundred yards north of the Clifton Upper Works plant around 1856. It wasn't stated, but it's believed that Crescent acquired the brickmaking facilities left behind by the Clifton Upper Works.

The plant consisted of two nine-foot drying pans, a twelve-foot pug mill, and a Freese auger machine with a capacity of 50,000 bricks. It also had a ten-track tunnel drier, and eight downdraft circular kilns approximately 28 feet in diameter.

Aetna or Etna Brick Plant

The Aetna Brick Plant, as it was formerly known, started in 1844 and later changed to just Etna. It was located about one-eighth of a mile north of the Crescent brickyard and about one-quarter mile south of the Eagle brickyard, which started operations in 1870.

This plant consisted of two nine-foot drying pans, a twelve-foot pug mill, and a Freese auger machine with a capacity of 50,000 bricks. It also had a ten-track tunnel drier and eight downdraft circular kilns approximately 28 feet in diameter.

Cunningham Brick Plant

The Cunningham Brick Plant was also started in 1844 and built north of the Etna plant and slightly south of where the Eagle plant was built. Little information was available regarding this plant other than it was relatively small and burned down around 1881.

Eagle Brick and Sewer Pipe Plant

The Eagle Brick and Sewer Pipe Plant started in 1870, two years after the Union Plant was started, and was located just one-quarter mile north. This plant incorporated the latest in sewer pipe making machinery. Beginning as a brick plant, it was quickly converted to a sewer pipe plant using Clarion clay that was dug very close to the plant.

The plant consisted of a nine-foot drying pan and a nine-foot wet pan. Clay was molded in a Turner Vaughn and Taylor press, with a 44-inch steam cylinder and 20-inch clay cylinder capable of making pipe from 2 to 24 inches in diameter. The pipe was dried on three sets of floors, one above the other, heated by steam and burned in eleven beehive downdraft kilns, 28 and 30 feet in diameter.

Union Brick Plant

The Union Brick Plant started in 1868 and was located about one-quarter of a mile north of the Eagle plant. It, like the Eagle plant, was equipped with the latest in brickmaking machinery.

This plant incorporated seven of the newer Eu Daly downdraft kilns and four conventional round downdraft kilns, all 28 feet in diameter and holding 34,000 paving blocks or 62,000 standard size bricks. It had a nine-foot drying pan, a pug mill, and a Freese auger machine.

This plant, like most in the area, dug clay directly near the plant. Union clay mine was considered the largest of all mines in the area and was exceptional in the way that clay was tipped directly into the clay processing building.

Rockyside Brick Plant

The Rockyside Brick Plant started in 1870 about the same time as the Eagle plant. This plant was situated approximately one-quarter mile north of the Union plant and about one-half mile south of the first Globe plant.

Rockyside plant incorporated three nine-foot drying pans, a pug mill, and a Freese auger machine. Bricks were dried in a nine-track tunnel drier and burned in ten Eu Daly downdraft kilns and two conventional round downdraft kilns all 28 feet in diameter.

Clay was brought into the plant from two mines located just above the plant and dropped into the drying pans. The brick was buff in color and on demand could be repressed on a Richardson machine.

Globe Brick Plant

The first Globe Brick Plant was initially the property of Standard Fire Brick Company that started in 1874 about one-half mile north of the Rockyside plant and about two and three-quarter miles north of New Cumberland. It was situated at the bottom of Globe Hill, the road that descends from the Rockyside hillside as you are traveling north.

Clay to this plant was mined directly above it and at the top of the hill. No tipple was ever erected, so the clay needed to be manually carried down to the bottom of the plant by cars. Once the clay reached the plant, it was broken in a Blake crusher and then finely ground in two nine-foot Stevenson drying pans before being transferred into a twelve-foot pug mill. The clay was then molded in a Bonnot stiff-mud auger machine which had a capacity of 60,000 bricks per day.

The bricks were dried in an eight-track hot air tunnel drier that had a capacity of 55,000 bricks. Then the bricks were burned in seven 28 foot and four 30-foot diameter kilns, all fired with coal. Each kiln could hold 50,000 and 60,000 bricks.

This brick was also buff in color. The plant ground approximately 200 to 300 tons of clay per month that was shipped to the steel works in Pittsburgh, PA.

Now let's take a look at how one plant operated specifically and how the books were kept for those men who worked in either the mines or the brickyards.

A Look Back at the Rockyside Brick Plant

I was extremely fortunate that George Hines, many years earlier, had the wisdom and foresight to gather four mine payroll journals that might have otherwise been discarded and destroyed. He took three of the four journals to a bookstore and bindery in Cincinnati, Ohio, and used his own money to have the books rebound. The fourth is yet to be rebound.

These journals are available to the public by contacting George to arrange a time to review them. They are secured at the old New Cumberland City Building where George has transformed the hallways into a museum dedicated to the history of the area. You can literally spend several hours looking at the history of New Cumberland as well as all of the photos of graduates from the old New Cumberland High School up to 1963 before the school consolidation occurred.

These books proved invaluable to me as I explored their pages which had kept their physical integrity for over 100 years. Even the one journal that was severely water damaged had pages that were in excellent condition. The handwriting must have been that of a female whose job it was to keep accurate accounts of each and every man employed at the company. (The reason I suggest it was a female is the smoothness of the penmanship. *I could be mistaken.*)

It took a lot of time to search each volume for any sign of my grandfathers. It dawned on me after several days of tirelessly searching, that a pattern had formed on these pages. It appeared that some of the last names were spelled phonetically. There were no first names for John. John was listed as "Jno." Names like Stolarczyk were spelled "Stolarchick." But after catching on as to how the information was being entered, I was surprised to find the names of both grandfathers and when they started in the brickyard.

These books clearly were inscribed with the identification of the Mack Manufacturing Company and the plants they owned back in 1901. The plants were Rockyside, Union, Etna, Eagle, Crescent, Clifton, and Sligo.

The company that George used did a beautiful job of binding. Also unique was the quality of the paper used inside each book. It had to be an extremely high quality paper to have lasted all these years.

Three bound payroll journals from Mack Manufacturing from the left 1901-1903, middle 1910-1912, and right 1912-1914
Books courtesy of George Hines

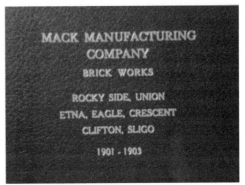

Photo of 1901 – 1903 journal cover
Photo courtesy of George Hines and T. W. Zielinsky

The binding company did an exceptional job keeping all the pages intact while recreating and attaching the hard covers to the book. There remains one final book that needs to be rebound, and hopefully that will happen soon. Now I will highlight and describe how each book looked inside.

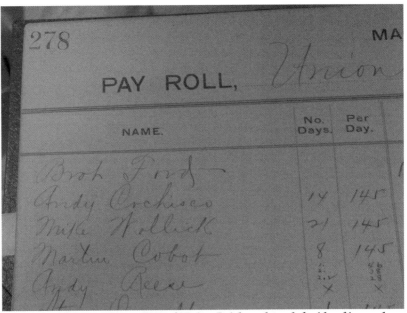

Payroll Journal page 278 of Union Brickyard top left side of journal

This first section is the left page, showing page 278, Pay Roll for the Union Works and shows the actual entries for that month and year.

Payroll Journal page 278 of Union Brickyard top middle of journal

This next section of page 278 shows the other entry columns coming across the page moving from left to right.

Payroll Journal page 278 of Union Brickyard top right side of journal
Three photos courtesy of George Hines and T. W. Zielinsky

This last section, or right side of the page, shows the remaining columns for June 1903 for the Union Works. Below is a written description of each section.

The following format was used throughout each journal. I took the format from the books and recreated it in a more simplistic way so you can see what each page contained. Notice also the penmanship. Someone took exceptional time, neatly entering names and amounts for each brickyard and mine.

Mack Manufacturing Payroll Journals Information

Each book contains 300 pages, 52 lines per page, with each page being 16 ¾" L by 13" W.

At the top of each page was the following:
Payroll _____ Works, for ____ 19 ____.

As an example, it would read:
Payroll Rocky Side Works or Mine, for December 1901.

The underlined portion was hand written and was consistent with the left side page for the Works and the right-side page for its associated clay mine.

Directly below the header was imprinted the following: Name, No. Days, Per Day, Amount, Deductions (Rent, Coal, Sundries), Total, Store, Bal Due & Paid, Remarks. As an example, it would look something like this:

Name	No. Days	Per Day	Amount	Deductions (Rent, Coal, Sundries)	Total	Store	Bal. Due	Paid	Remarks

Under the deductions column, items would include Rent, Coal, and Sundries. I am not sure exactly what sundries were in that time. Also, there is a column for store items, and most employees appeared to have had credit at the store. The Mack Company built a company store at Pearl and North Chestnut Street in 1890 that was later converted to a fully functional general store. The name was changed several times, but it was often referred to as the People's Store or the A&S Food Store. This building was actually built sometime around 1890 or before, because the building is shown on the Sanborn Insurance Map Company drawings as of 1890. Then on the 1897 map, the building is referenced to as The Mack Manufacturing Company. So sometime between 1897 and 1903, when miners were given credit on the payroll journals, is about when a general store went into operation.

BUILT BY MACK CO. AS COMPANY STORE ABOUT 1906.
Photo of the A&S Food Store on the corner of Pearl and Chestnut
Photo courtesy of The Brick and Clay Record, page 116

Book 1 was dated from December 1901 to June 1903.
Book 2 was dated from August 1910 to October 1912
Book 3 was dated from November 1912 to December 1914

The unbound book was from July 1903 to October 1905. This book is earmarked to have covers done for it as well.

Each book was identical in layout and never varied. The brickyard was listed on the left-hand page, and the associated clay mine was listed on the right-hand page.

I took the number of employees working in 1901 and then compared them to those working in 1914. The number of people working varied only slightly. Mack held a steady number of workers despite having to close several plants. The following number of employees working at the various brickyard operations in December 1901 was as follows:

Works	Number of Employees
Rockyside Works	25
Rockyside Mine	22
Union Works	15
Union Mine	13
Eagle Works	1
Eagle Mine	7
Etna Works	55
Etna Mine	16
Crescent Works	61
Crescent Mine	24
Clifton Works	70
Clifton Mine	12
Sligo Works	60
Sligo Mine	9
	390
Miscellaneous	19
Stables	2
Store	3
Barracks	3
Office	7
Club House	1
	35
Total Employees	**425**

These last 6 entries were listed on a Recapitulation Sheet
Data is from December 1901

In February of 1903, both the Eagle Works and the Eagle Mine were operational, but in March both the works and mine were closed. The Sligo works was closed in May 1904, and in August 1904 the Clifton Works was closed.

The number of men varied from month to month. Some men worked for years in the same place at either the brick and sewer pipe works or the mines. As an example, on January 1902, employment and a day's wages were as follows:

Men in the works earned $1.35 per day. Men in the mines either earned $1.00 per day or averaged $0.16 to $0.25 per hour of work. In October 1913, Mack Company began taking out for insurance, either $.05 or $.09 from the paychecks. No additional information was available, and no record was found as to what type of insurance was being provided.

Married men living in a company house had $2.00 per month deducted from their pay for rent. Single men living in the barracks had $0.50 per day deducted from their pay for room and board.

The total number of employees in January 1902 was 386 and 32 in staff/office and maintenance positions. That level kept consistent each year. As the works or mines worked themselves out, the number of employees went down as well.

I was extremely fortunate that the books that I reviewed had information about my immediate family and relatives. I also discovered several interesting bookkeeping traits that were used. Whoever kept the books entered and spelled some of the last names phonically. As an example, my uncle Joseph Stolarczyk was spelled Stolarchick (Sto – lar – chick). Also interesting was that for some strange reason John was never spelled, but entered as Jno. So it took a while to find certain names, but after going through these very large books several dozen times I was able to locate a majority of my family.

Also interesting to note was that nearly all last names ending in (i) were changed to (y). However, first names were closely matched to their actual first name; an example is Vincent Zukoski was entered as Vincenty Zukoski. My grandfather Zielinski's name was spelled as Jno (John) Zalensky, and my other grandfather Jno (John) Zömer's name was eventually changed to John Zumer.

Using John Zumer as an example, I followed his journey through Rockyside and was truly surprised at what I found. The payroll journals indicated the dates when he actually started and stopped working at Rockyside.

My grandfather Zumer started in June 1903 at the Union brickyard and worked there three months. In September 1903, he began work at the Union Mine and worked until April 1904 when he began work at the Rockyside Mine.

Then he worked at the Crescent Mine in May of 1904, and the Etna Mine in June 1904. Apparently, he moved wherever he could get work. In 1905, he spent most of his time at the Rockyside Mine. Then in December 1914, he went back and worked in the Union Mine until being crushed on October 19, 1926. His untimely death happened one day before my mother's fourteenth birthday.

Here is an example and sample of what was listed in Book 1.

Mack Manufacturing Payroll Journal 1901 – 1903 Book 1

Book 1	Page	Line	Name	Hours	Rate	Total
	28	10	Jno Baginsky	7	$1.35	$9.45
February 1902 Etna Works						
	245	3	Vicenty Zukoski	21 ½	$1.45	$31.17
June 1903 Union Works						
	278	9	Jno Zomer	40.2 4 13.7	$0.46 $0.28 $0.28	$23.84
June 1903 Union Works – Grandfather John Zumer began working on Rockyside						

When I entered all the amounts from the journal and added them together, it seemed a little odd. If you look closely, my grandfather's total wages were in error by $0.39 in his favor. I was also able to find my grandfather's name by searching each entry from 1901 to 1903. The next photo is how my grandfather's name first appeared in the payroll journal on June 1903 when he started working at the Union Works.

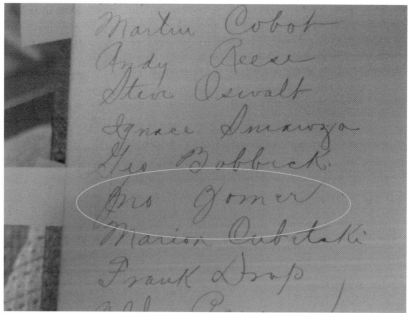

Photo of Jno Zomer's name from payroll journal 1901 – 1903 entered on page 278, line 9 – started working at the Union Works in June 1903 and earned a total of $23.84 for the month
Photo courtesy of T. W. Zielinsky and George Hines

I've compiled information on a number of other miners and brickyard workers in the following examples, showing how work was calculated from 1901 to 1914. These books are available for review but require prior approval by George Hines by contacting him at the New Cumberland City Building.

My dad's father Valentine Zielinski can be found on the next page, but his name was written as Votsy Zalensky. He started working on Rockyside in August 1910. Prior to this time, my grandfather worked in the various coal mines. Coal was the primary fuel used to fire the kilns. He would later leave the brickyard and go back to digging coal.

Book 2	Page	Line	Name	Hours	Rate	Total
	2	24	Jno Zomer	24	$1.75	$42.00
August 1910 Rockyside Mine						
	49	25	Votsy Zalensky	2	$1.60	$3.20
December 1910 Crescent Mine						
	67	45	Julian Chetock	4	$1.60	$6.40
February 1911 Union Works – $1.00 was deducted for rent.						
	178	45	Votsy Zalensky	14	$1.60	$22.40
December 1911 Rockyside Works - $20 was deducted for the store.						
	265	29	Jno Zomer	4	$1.60	$6.40
August 2912 Union Works						
	276	15	Alex Zukosky	21 ¾ 2.5	$2.00 $0.45	$48.55
September 1912 Rockyside Works						

It is unclear how payroll journaling was done prior to 1901 at the other brickyards, especially south of New Cumberland. Nothing was found to show who worked in the early brickyards and clay mines or how hours and wages were recorded before 1894. It was only when the Mack Manufacturing Company purchased Rockyside, Union, Eagle, Etna, Crescent, Clifton, and Sligo plants under a consolidation in 1894 that professional records, in these large bound journals, can be identified.

Book 3	Page	Line	Name	Hours	Rate	Total
	2	15	Jno Zomer	24 ½	$1.75	$42.87
November 1912 Rockyside Mine – Deductions $2 rent, $4.50 coal, $35 at the store – total pay $1.37 for the month.						
	11	32	Joseph Stolarchick	5	$1.60	$8.00
December 1912 Rockyside Works						
	66	11	Gregory Spilitsky	19	$1.85	$35.15
May 1913 Crescent Works						
	275	46	Vadislof Charnetsky	37 ½	$.28	$10.50
November 1914 Crescent Works – Deductions $5.10 sundries, $5.00 store, $.05 insurance – total pay $.35 for the month.						
	278	15	Paul Baginsky	1	$1.75	$1.75
December 1914 Rockyside Works – Deduction of $.05 for insurance						
	279	8	Starvy Chetock	9 .6	$.45 $.35	$4.26
December 1914 Rockyside Works – Deduction of $.05 for insurance						
	281	3	Jno Zomer	21	$1.75	$36.75
December 1914 Union Mine – Deductions $3.00 rent, $6.00 coal, $25.00 store, $.05 insurance – total pay $2.70 for the month.						

Book 4	Page	Line	Name	Hours	Rate	Total
This book needs recovered and is in reasonable shape with most pages intact. This book starts July 1903 through October 1905.						

In comparison to 1901, the following number of employees working at the various brickyard operations in November 1914 was as follows.

Works	Number of Employees
Rockyside Works	75
Rockyside Mine	24
Union Works	62
Union Mine	25
Eagle Works	Closed
Eagle Mine	Closed
Etna Works	74
Etna Mine	22
Crescent Works	72
Crescent Mine	28
Clifton Works	Closed
Clifton Mine	Closed
Sligo Works	Closed
Sligo Mine	Closed
	382
Miscellaneous	17
Stables	2
Store	1
Barracks	4
Office	9
Club House	Closed
Clifton Works	1
Sligo Works	2
	36
Total Employees	**418**

These last 8 entries were listed on a Recapitulation Sheet
Data is from November 1914

Despite a span of nearly fourteen years, the average employment held nearly steady, losing only seven employees. This loss of seven employees is with the closing of Eagle, Clifton, and Sligo operations. Security guards were added to Clifton and Sligo after those facilities closed to protect the property. Also from 1901 until early 1914, wages for workers saw only a modest increase. Each facility was within a few cents of one another in terms of hourly rates, with increases from $1.35 to roughly $1.75 per hour. These were hourly rates for the mineworkers, and they were consistent across all operating mines. Rates for brickyard workers were slightly higher, starting around $1.75 and increasing to $2.75 over the fourteen-year period.

Finally, I was curious as to the monthly amount workers made during this period of time. I selected my grandfather Jno Zomer and compiled his earnings and expenses from January 1913 to December 1913 – they were as follows:

Jno Zomer payroll earnings beginning January 1913

Month	Earnings	Store	Rent	Coal	Ins.	Total
Jan	$43.50	$22.00	$2.00	$3.00	$0	$16.50
Feb	$47.00	$39.00	$2.00	$3.00	$0	$3.00
Mar	$35.00	$25.00	$2.00	$0	$0	$8.00
April	$49.00	$33.00	$2.00	$3.00	$0	$11.00
May	$50.00	$33.00	$2.00	$0	$0	$15.00
June	$48.00	$32.00	$2.00	$0	$0	$14.00
July	$56.50	$35.00	$2.00	$0	$0	$19.50
Aug	$48.00	$27.00	$2.00	$0	$0	$19.00
Sept	$50.00	$32.00	$2.00	$3.00	$0	$13.00
Oct	$53.00	$30.00	$2.00	$3.00	$0.05	$17.95
Nov	$43.00	$30.00	$2.00	$3.00	$0.05	$7.95
Dec	$37.00	$29.00	$2.00	$3.00	$0.05	$2.95
Totals	**$560.00**	**$367.00**	**$24.00**	**$21.00**	**$0.15**	**$147.85**

As you can see from the table, in 1913 my grandfather earned a total of $560.00 for the entire year and had $147.85 left over to support a family of six. The household consisted of a mother, father, three children, and a new baby just three months old at the start of the year, my mother.

The cost of living in the early 1903 was very cheap compared to today's prices. A loaf of bread was $.05, a dozen eggs was $.21, a pound of steak was $.12, a pound of bacon was $.13, a ten-pound bag of potatoes was $.14, coffee was $.35 a pound, and 5 lbs. of flour was $.12.

Prices ten years later in 1913 were just about the same with some products edging upward a penny or two, but relatively the same. Gas in 1913 was just $.12 a gallon. Most families living on Rockyside had cows and chickens and planted a garden in the summer. They made their own cheese and bread, so items that needed to be purchased were limited.

Some of the names found in those payroll journals have been listed below. I would encourage anyone interested in their family history to make it a point to search through these books.

Names that might be familiar to New Cumberland who once worked the brickyards and mines

Allison	Bagienski	Baxter	Boyles
Bradley	Budno	Burskey	Chetock
Cullen	Cuppy	Dunlevy	Evans
Fadaley	Fickes	Gehring	Glover
Gordon	Hoder	Jacobs	Knox
Long	Manypenny	McNickols	Narkevich
Reese	Robb	Robertson	Roseberry
Salisbury	Spelicki	Staley	Stewart
Swearingen	Sweat	Tate	Thayer
Troop	Troup	Turley	Turoff
Uker	Wells	Zielinsky	Zubrycki
Zucosky	Zumer		

Brick production rapidly increased in 1890 to over 96,188,000 bricks. 88,652,000 bricks were shipped to the cities of Cleveland, Philadelphia, Steubenville, and Wheeling. Philadelphia alone received 64,390,000 bricks in that year. Between 1890 and 1905 more than 323,588,000 bricks were shipped to 15 major cities and Washington, D.C. Production was averaging 21,516,000 bricks annually.[4]

Chapter Seven
The First Catholic Church and School in New Cumberland

 What was extremely important to me was my hope of finding a picture of the first Catholic Church in New Cumberland. Up to the point of starting my research, no picture of this church could be found. John Kuzio remembered all too well his early days as an altar server when he was just seven years old. He remembers climbing the hill up to the Zumer home, crossing Route 66, and climbing yet another hill to get to the church.

He remembered very clearly the Zumer home, sitting on the left side of the road going north, as the only large wooden home situated along that steep hill that overlooked the brickyard. He remembered being able to stand on the porch and throw a rock and hit the top of the brick kiln directly below.

I remembered my father telling the story of how on Sunday mornings he would get to ring the bell at the church as a signal mass was getting ready to start and how the sound of the bell could be heard up and down the Ohio River Valley.

My problem taking on this project was that there weren't a lot of people around who remembered what Rockyside once looked like, and I surely didn't know of anyone specifically who had pictures. First, I needed people who might have pictures, and then realized I didn't know that many people. But that all changed after a number of articles about my search appeared in local newspapers. It seems some people do still read newspapers, and people who saw the article started calling.

Not only did I talk to John Kuzio, but I also contacted Pam Riggi at the Immaculate Conception Church about any information that might exist on the history of the church. Pam was kind enough to offer me the church documents, but those didn't have what I was looking for. I contacted the office of the Wheeling-Charleston Dioceses and spoke with a Mr. Jon-Erik Gilot, Director of Archives and Records. He was able to provide me with a newspaper article from 1904 that described how Immaculate Conception began as a mission church, but he unfortunately didn't have any photos. The only picture of this church (really not a picture) was a drawing that Mr. Steve Kuzio, John's brother, made for a church publication used in the dedication of the current church on Ridge Avenue on Sunday, May 4, 1969. No other documents could be found.

John Kuzio described the little wooden white church as being built into the hillside, having several windows on either side, with the front door facing toward the river. Those coming out of church could view the massive beauty of the Ohio River. The church also had a small steeple that contained the bell that welcomed those getting ready to attend mass. He also remembered that the church had one large main altar in the center of the back wall, with two smaller side altars on either side of the main altar. There of course was no heat in the building.

Using the only picture I had of the assumed Zumer home, I found what looked like a faint steeple in the sky, up on the hillside behind the house. Using a Fitbit (device used to measure how many steps you take in a day) and an application on my iPhone, I found that the Zumer home was located approximately one-half mile south on Route 66, measured from the site of the existing overlook. I also knew that if I was correct, and it was the steeple to the church, the foundation should be located several yards farther south from that distance.

Walking and using the Fitbit and iPhone app as my guide, I traveled south on Route 2 approximately one-half mile, and then proceeded into the hillside. Walking as straight as I could south about 50-yards, I spotted an indention in the hillside. To my amazement, I found where the church was built. The area consisted of large sections of sewer pipe still filled with brick and dirt inserted into the ground. Many pieces of brick, both large and small, lay scattered over the ground. And finally, many pieces of dark gray and black slate lay in various places over this area as well.

Of course, there were also many large and medium size trees and heavy brush that had overtaken this area; after all it was over a hundred years since anyone, other than hunters, had walked here. Stomping down as much as I could, without killing myself, I tried to clear a spot so it would be easier to find the next day. I took a few photos and called George Hines.

The next day George and I found the spot, and he agreed this definitely was where the church was located. We did more stomping, and armed with yellow caution tape, laid out the perimeter, as best we could, again without killing ourselves. With such thick underbrush, our feet got easily tangled. I came out a couple of times a bloody mess. We ended up taking more photos, which now better reflected the true area of where this first Catholic Church of New Cumberland once stood. George also found a glass bottle, perfectly intact, with a date of 1903 that he was going to do some research on as to where it might have originated.

I saw Jim Zucosky about a week later after church services at Sacred Heart of Mary in Weirton. Jim's father Alex had passed away a few years earlier and was very good friends with my father's family. The Zielinsky and Zucosky families actually lived next door in the same house on Rockyside. Jim stated he discovered an old photo album that had a picture of a church, and he thought I might be interested.

After receiving the album, I was excited to find a couple of pictures that were taken on Rockyside, but I was not familiar with the location. There was also a picture of a small white church against a hillside, but something about it looked a little odd to me. Taking a copy up to John Kuzio to look over, I was surprised when John said he thought it might be the church, but was not one hundred percent sure. It turned out that it wasn't the church, and my suspicions were correct. I noticed a lot of trees, and especially pine trees, that circled the little church. I noticed that pine trees are not plentiful on Rockyside, so this, without a doubt, could not be the church.

It wasn't until several weeks later, after one of my articles ran in a local paper, that I received an email from a friend saying that she might have a picture, but she was still searching. One week later, another email arrived, but this one was a huge surprise; the church, at last!

So, another copy was made of this church and another road trip to see John Kuzio. Hopefully he might recognize this picture of a small wooden white church. John without reservation said that yes, this is the church. You can tell, by the brief description I gave of this area, this is Rockyside. There is not a tree insight, and the church is carved back into and sits against the hillside. The exact impression of what George and I found several weeks earlier.

I owe an extreme debt of gratitude to Dave and Bonnie Burskey for finding this picture. It was Dave's aunt, Eleanor Burskey, who as a teacher at the one-room Rockyside schoolhouse, somehow captured this picture. The picture was located with old photos she kept in a box that Dave and Bonnie took possession of after she passed away. This is the only picture that currently exists of this first church. There might be other pictures, but this is the only one that has come forward.

The first Immaculate Conception Catholic Church built 1904 on Rockyside
Photo Courtesy of Dave and Bonnie Burskey[1]

How this church came to exist is outlined in an article I received from Mr. Jon-Erik Gilot from the Dioceses of Wheeling-Charleston. This article appeared in a Catholic publication called *The Church Calendar* that was printed to keep parishioners informed about events within and around the dioceses. This publication preceded the current monthly publication called *The Catholic Spirit*.

The article will be transcribed at the back of the book in the Photo Section. In part, the article describes how Right Rev. Bishop Patrick Donahue traveled to the northern panhandle to see what could be done for the spiritual needs of the Poles and Slavs who were employed in that area. The Bishop indicated that he appointed Rev. Julius Javorek pastor of the new mission. Father Javorek had just recently been ordained and spoke nothing but Polish. He was assigned to stay with a Mrs. Kelly who had extended gracious hospitality to visiting clergy. The unusual problem was that Father Javorek spoke no English, and Mrs. Kelly spoke no Polish.

The Church Calendar Publication 09/1904
Document Courtesy of Dioceses of Wheeling-Charleston[2]

The Mack Company gave the Bishop the property and material and assisted the men in the building of this church. This situation was unique in that the church construction began in September 1904 and was completed four months later when the church was dedicated, December 24, 1904, on Christmas Eve. The part of the church unfinished was the steeple and the hanging of the bell, which occurred in early spring.

Based on extrapolation, the church measured roughly 20 feet wide by 40 feet long and was made entirely from wood. These numbers are based on assuming the steps up to the front door are approximately four feet wide. The church contained a main altar at the center back wall and two smaller side altars on either side. There was no heat source in the building.

Church records show that on November 12, 1904, Mr. Jan (John) Zumer and Victoria Dobosz were married in this church. John and Victoria were my grandparents on my mother's side.

Church records also show this church, Immaculate Conception, started out as a mission church of Sacred Heart of Mary in Chester, WV. By 1907, it was also a mission of St. Anthony's in Follansbee, WV, and by 1911 a mission of St. Paul's in Weirton, WV. The church became a parish in its own right in 1920.

In 1920, the Rev. Father Francis Olszewski was appointed pastor of the Immaculate Conception Church, by the Most Reverend Patrick Donahue, Bishop of Wheeling, WV. Father Olszewski came to this area from the Fargo Diocese of North Dakota and held services on this hillside for the next 14 years.

Nuns accompanied Father Olszewski from an order he started when he lived in Edmonton, Canada, before locating to North Dakota. The nuns were known as the Sisters Auxiliaries of the Apostolate and were housed in Monongah, WV.

In 1921 Father Olszewski started the Immaculate Conception Catholic School. This parochial school was located on North River Avenue and was comprised of two classrooms situated on the first floor. These rooms, looking at the front of the building, were on the right side. A large room at the back right of the building would serve as the first-grade classroom, and an equally large classroom at the front right would serve as classroom for second through eighth grade, with each row of seats being a different grade. A large potbelly coal stove sat approximately in the middle between these two rooms.

On the left side of the building were rooms for the two nuns. A kitchen at the back of the building faced the river, and a sitting room with piano was at the front. It was on that piano that I first started taking music lessons. Little did I know it would lead to accordion lessons when I was nine years old.

The second floor contained a small chapel on the left at the top of the stairs and bedrooms located over the classrooms on the right side of the building.

This building was formerly a hotel/boarding house when purchased by Father Olszewski in 1921. It was later deeded to the Sisters Auxiliaries of Apostolate in 1923 along with the Wheeling Dioceses. In 1938, the Sisters took full possession listing 6 members (nuns) on the deed.

School was started shortly after Father bought the building and made some renovations, with the first class (eighth grade) graduating in 1922.

I attended grades 1, 2 and 3 from 1952 to 1955. Father Olszewski passed away on February 24, 1955. We completed our respective grades, and then the school was closed. All students then attended New Cumberland Public School.

Father Matthias S. Nemec, Father Olszewski's replacement, purchased the property in 1955 until my Uncle Fred R. Mack purchased it in 1959. Uncle Fred kept the property until 1980 when he had the building torn down.

The building was unique in that it had no running water. Water was obtained from a well in the back-center courtyard. The courtyard was made entirely from bricks. At the far left and right corners of the courtyard (toward the river) stood matching his and hers outhouses. Heat was provided by a series of coal stoves; one in the center that served both classrooms, and a small one in the upstairs bedroom area. Of course, the kitchen had a traditional coal stove used to prepare meals, and this kept the left side of the building warm. It was great going to school there. Now, those were the "good old days."

Chapter Eight
Other Manufacturing in New Cumberland

There were several manufacturing companies in New Cumberland besides brick that many people didn't realize had ever existed. These include; the Chelsea China Company, the New Cumberland Glass Works, the Cutler Steel/Duraloy Company, and the Hancock County Manufacturing Company.

Hancock County Manufacturing - 1849

The history of this plant begins in 1849 when it was established and operated by Isaac Wheeler as a stove foundry and was located at Taylor and South Chester Streets. In 1880, it was acquired by J. O. Miller and operated as the Shetter Foundry and Machine Company. Ten years later, it was bought by the Davis-Price Foundry and Machine Company and operated until 1925.[2] Alfred H. Chapman moved his machine works into the building in 1930 and renamed the business the Chapman Foundry and Machine Company. Ten years later, the business was renamed the Hancock County Manufacturing[1] and Stamping plant. Matthew Phillips purchased the foundry in 1944 and renamed it the New Cumberland Metal Products Company, under the M&E Company.

The M&E Company was owned and operated by Matthew and Edward Phillips. The Matthew Phillips Company also owned not only the Metal Products plant that supplied television and radio parts, but Phillips Lumber and Supply, Phillips Hardware and Supply, and the Phillips Coal and Clay Company. The company officials were: Matthew Phillips, president; Minnie Phillips, vice president; and Ferne Manack, secretary-treasurer.

New Cumberland Metals Products closed in 1970. The property was purchased by the Barkhurst Construction Company of Weirton, WV, and is in the process of being demolished.

Photo of the Davis-Price Foundry and Machine Company 1889 – photo shows front of foundry facing the Ohio River. Foundry was located at Taylor and Water Streets currently South River Avenue.
Photo Courtesy of Ohio Valley Manufacturer

Photo of the New Cumberland Metal Products Company – photo shows the back of the building facing S. Chester Street and was taken August 17, 1947
Photo courtesy of Hancock County Courier

Chelsea China Company - 1889

Another early business that was built in town was the Chelsea China[1] plant that was started in 1889 by none other than Mr. John Porter. This plant was located at the south end of New Cumberland at the end of South Chester Street. At the far southern end, a road was constructed and named Chelsea Hill. This road intersected with Ridge Avenue.

Chelsea China Company – Stone, China and Decorated Ware[2]
Photo Courtesy of Hancock County Courier

The building and property were developed in just over one year. The entire building was constructed of over 1,500,000 firebricks. For the foundation, 2,200 perches of stone were required to support the structure. The lower walls were eighteen inches thick, and the upper walls were thirteen inches thick. Eight kilns, sixteen and one-half feet in diameter and fifty feet high, were installed. The power for the building was furnished by a 130-horse power Corliss engine. The building contained eighteen different departments; in each department, a different part of the production work was completed. The building covered a full acre of ground, contained 620 windows, and the ventilation was as near perfect as possible.

The plant was rebuilt after it was hit by a major fire in 1894. The Union Pottery Company took ownership of the plant around 1904, and three years later the plant was again destroyed by fire. During this period, ownership changed hands several times while the plant was being rebuilt. Around 1910, the plant was sold to United States Electric Porcelain Company, a division of Superior Porcelain Company, and then sold to Standard Porcelain in 1911. During these ownership changes, the name of the plant changed as well. The building sat idle for many years until around 1920, when the name of the plant changed back to Chelsea China Company. After only a few years of operation, in 1926 the plant came under control of the Cronin Brothers of East Liverpool, OH. They ran the plant until 1930 when it ceased operation. The plant was destroyed by floodwaters in 1936 and never rebuilt.

New Cumberland Glass Works - 1891

There was also a New Cumberland Glass Works[1] plant that was started around 1890 to the north of the Chelsea China Company. This plant remained open until 1930 when it was destroyed by fire and never rebuilt.

Cutler Steel – Duraloy Company - 1920

The Cutler Steel/Duraloy Company was located along North Chestnut Street about where the Sparkle Market is currently located. The company had a very interesting background. I was fortunate to have contacted Mr. Vince Schiavoni, the current president of Duraloy Industries, who provided me with the history of company. The history was outlined and documented in a book authored by Mr. Thomas R. Heyward, Jr., the founder. I decided to place some of the history of this company in the Photo Section under Chapter Eight. It is well worth reading.

Cutler Steel Company (foundry) of New Cumberland, WV, was organized as The Cutler Steel Company of Pittsburgh and was incorporated under the laws of Delaware. This plant was built in 1916 and produced steel castings with an annual capacity of about 10,000 tons. It was initially owned by the National Steel Casting Company until the Heyward Steel Company of Pittsburgh organized a take-over in 1918. Then in August 1919, the plant was acquired by Thomas R. Heyward,

Jr. It came into full operation in 1921 and produced alloy steel bars (stainless steel), billets, and high carbon sheets. The stainless steel was used to make cutlery, hence the name Cutler Steel. The building was devastated by the 1936 flood and became idle. The following year, February 1937, the plant was completely destroyed by fire and was never rebuilt. The fire was so devastating that only the portions of the outside walls were left standing. The roof, kilns, and wall facing the river were taken to the ground. The remnants of this building were left standing for more than 20 years, and the area became overgrown with weeds and trees. It was eventually demolished when the property was renovated for a new store to replace the aging A&S/People's store.

As amazing as it might seem, a steel foundry that started making the first stainless steel cutlery products in 1921 still exists today in Scottdale, PA, after over 80 years in existence. *New Cumberland, so rich in what it once contributed to the world.*

Foundry at New Cumberland, W. Va.   1921 - 1937

The picture[2] courtesy of Duraloy President Vince Schiavoni representing Mr. Thomas Rhett Heyward, Jr., founder and owner of the company

Chapter Nine
The Zumer and Zielinsky Families

I wanted to include a chapter dedicated to the Zumer and Zielinsky families. If it hadn't been for these individuals coming from Europe, working in the brick and clay mines, finding each other, getting married, and starting families, I wouldn't be here writing this book.

As a tribute to their hard work and sacrifices, I dedicate a small section that reflects who they were and where they came from. I cannot for the life of me know what these families must have endured living on that hillside for nearly 20 years before moving into the town of New Cumberland. They had practically no conveniences at all.

Growing up, I never met or knew my mother's mother or father, but from looking at these and other photos of my grandmother, my mother Walda was a spitting image of her mother.

Photos of Grandmother Victoria (Dobusz) Zumer 12/23/1884 – 4/15/1943
Grandfather Jan (John) Zömer Zumer 5/17/1877 – 10/19/1926

The Zömer (Zumer) Family

Victoria Dobush (12/23/1884 – 4/15/1943) – Grandmother
Janusz Jan (John) Zömer (5/17/1877 – 10/19/1926) –
Grandfather – Married (11/12/1904)

> Children – **Mary (1905 – 1996)**
>> Husband – Joseph Stolarczyk (d1973)
>> Children; Darlene (d2014),
>> Josephine (d2004), Sophie (d2003),
>> Teddy, Emily, Virginia, Helene.
>
> **Josephine (1907 – 2002)**
>> Husband – James Reese (d1995)
>> Children; Gertrude, Marjorie (d2016)
>
> **Verna (1911 – 1998)**
>> Husband – Oral Knight (d1993)
>> Children; Donald (d2006),
>> Nancy, Charlotte
>
> **Walda (1912 – 1989)**
>> Husband – Walter Zielinsky (d1999)
>> Children; Tom, John (d2016), Donald
>
> **Jane (1916 – 1979)**
>> Husband – Joseph Chetock (d1971)
>> Children; Barbara, Linda (d2011), James
>
> **John (1918 – 2003)**
>> Wife; Mary Strunak (d1996)
>> Children; Richard, Ronnie, Mary Ann
>
> (d) *Indicates Year of Death*

Here is some basic genealogy on the start of the Zömer (Zumer) family: Grandfather John Zömer came from Poland. The only official record is a baptismal certificate for my mother Walda. Listed on this certificate is John Zömer, born in Kalisz, Poland. This town, of about 104,000 people, is near the west-central part of Poland as displayed on the map. His last name of Zömer was changed at some point while he was working in the brickyard or clay mine. The (o) with the 2 dots on top (ö) was dropped and made a (u). This letter in the Polish alphabet has a (u) sound anyway, so it was appropriate the name changed to reflect Zumer.

Grandmother Victoria Dobush (spelled Dobosz) on the same baptismal certificate was born in Galicia, Austria. In my

90

research, I found that Galicia was not a town but a kingdom back in the early 1900s. Records further show she came from a town called Sanok of the Kingdom of Galicia, but of Poland. This is where it gets a little hard to follow. This little county created a lot of confusion. As you can see in Photo 1, Galicia bordered the Kingdom of Poland to the north and the Austrian Empire to the south. Later this town became part of the southeastern part of Poland when land boundaries were reshuffled. Sanok has a population of roughly 40,000 people.

Map of the Kingdom of Galicia between Poland and Austria[1] – Photo 1

This county was primarily known as the Kingdom of Galicia and Lodomeria around 1846-1918, and then the countries split boundaries making way for Poland to acquire the territory for its southern borders. The next photo (Photo 2) shows where Galicia was in relation to today's countries.

As you can see in the photo, much of this land was predominately Ukraine, so the nationality of my grandmother was primarily Ukrainian with a sprinkling of Austrian and Polish. She still kept the old traditions of her homeland at Christmas and Easter.

Galicia as it relates to other bordering countries[1] – Photo 2

So with all this said, where does this leave us? The official account is that Sanok is a town in Poland, formally the town of the Kingdom of Galicia, Austria. While I was doing this research, John Kuzio mentioned that his father, John Kuzio, Sr., was born in the same town, Sanok (Galicia) Poland. *Small world indeed.*

The spelling of Dobush is also like all other eastern European names sometimes taking on two or more variations. The family adopted Dobush, but the actual baptismal certificate spells the name Dobosz. A handwritten note that I have from my mother spells her mother's name as Dobosz, the European spelling.

Map on the left showing the location of Sanok, Poland[2]
Map on the right showing the location of Kalisz, Poland[2]

Grandfather John Zumer was tragically killed in a mining accident inside the Union clay mine on Tuesday, October 19, 1926. He died one day before my mother's 14th birthday. The article in the *East Liverpool Review – Tribune* indicated that he was wedged between cars on the track near New Cumberland. The article went on to say he succumbed in the City Hospital from internal injuries.

He was a driver in the Union mine of the Crescent Brick Company. Apparently, the accident happened when he missed his footing and fell directly between two cars which were moving in opposite directions. He was removed to the East Liverpool hospital by Dr. F. P. Beaumont of New Cumberland.

He left behind his wife and six children. He was buried the very next day from the Polish church in New Cumberland (Rockyside) and was laid to rest in the New Cumberland Cemetery.

Despite the accidental death of my grandfather, mine records indicate that very few deaths actually occurred. Surprisingly, there were no death reports as a result of cave-ins or tunnel ceiling collapses.

Photo of front page headlines of East Liverpool Review – Tribune dated
October 20, 1926 – write up is in the right column
Photo courtesy of the East Liverpool Review

The Zielinsky Family

Barbara Hoder (12/8/1881 – 5/1/1957) – Grandmother
Valentine John (Valenty) (2/12/1897 – 7/28/1953) –
Grandfather – Married (5/26/1906)

    Children – **Mary (1907 – 1996)**
        Husband – Paul Bagienski (d1968)
        Children; Helen (d1987), Julia (d1996),
        Joseph (d2011)

        Catherine (Katie) – (1909 – 1997)
        Husband – Nick Nardo (d1991)
        Children; Nick, William, Gary

        Walter (1911 – 1999)
        Wife – Walda Zumer (d1989)
        Children; Tom, John (d2016), Donald

        Helen (1912 – 2004)
        Husband – Fred Mack (d1990)
        Children; Shirley (d2013)

        Joseph (1913 – 2000)
        Wife – Never Married
        Children; None

        Valentine (Baldy) (1914 – 1988)
        Wife – Helen Combs (died – date
        unknown)
        Children; Jeannie

        **Frank (1919 – 1944) France WWII,
        Killed in Action**
        Wife – None
        Children; None

        (d) *Indicates Year of Death*

I did know my grandparents on my father's side, but my grandfather died when I was just seven, so I really don't have a lot of memories of him. I do remember my grandmother and how she enjoyed me playing my accordion on the porch on Sundays. She would also make a special cabbage soup that was to die for, but only on special occasions. She cooked on a cast-iron stove fueled by either coal or wood.

Photos of Grandmother Barbara (Hoder) Zielinski 12/8/1881 – 5/1/1957
Grandfather Valentine (John) Zielinski 2/12/1897 – 7/28/1953
All photos courtesy of T. W. Zielinsky

Now here is some basic genealogy on the start of the Zielinski family: The only document (marriage license) found was located at the courthouse for Valentine Zielinski and Barbara Hoder, registered May 16, 1906. It showed his age as 27 and her age as 23, and they were both born in Austria. There was no town listed for either name. So it is unclear where exactly they were born. My dad always stated that his father was born in Poland near Krakow, and said his mother was born in Austria in the town of Graz. However, without some form of legal documentation, it cannot be confirmed.

Graz, Austria, is located in the southeastern corner of Austria and has a population of roughly 320,000 people. Krakow, Poland, on the other hand, is situated on southern part of Poland and has a population of nearly 760,000 people.

Map on the left shows the location of Graz, Austria[2]
Map on the right shows the location of Krakow, Poland[2]

Chapter Ten
A Tribute to Captain John S. Porter "Brick King"

Captain John Porter "Brick King"[1]

*J*ohn Porter, one of the most substantial and energetic businessmen of New Cumberland, WV, was born at Martin's Ferry, Ohio, August 7, 1838. His father, Moses Porter, was born in Ireland, and came to America when he was fifteen years of age. He resided in Wheeling, WV, and at different places in Pennsylvania, and followed the business of manufacturing brick.

In 1836, he came to Hancock County, WV., and began the manufacture of fire-brick, which he continued until his death in March, 1845. After the death of his father, John Porter made his home with his uncle, James Porter. He received his education in the common schools of Hancock County, and obtained the greater part of his instruction in the old time log school houses.

He was married in 1869 to Carrie A. Mahan, who was born in this county, the daughter of John L. and Barbara (Brenneman) Mahan, the former of whom was born in Baltimore, MD, September 17, 1814, and came to this county about 1830, and has since been one of the prominent citizen, and is a farmer by occupation.

Mrs. Porter's mother is a granddaughter of Jacob Nessly, one of the earliest settlers of this section. Mr. and Mrs. Porter are the parents of six children, of whom Lea, Virginia, Frederick G., James B. and Jacob Nessly are living, and John C. and William K. are deceased. They were all members of the Presbyterian Church.

Politically John was an ardent republican, but his extensive business interests have occupied his attention to such an extent that he has had but little time to devote to politics. Although Mr. Porter was left when young to make his own way in the world, he is now one of the leading manufacturers of the upper Ohio valley.

His first work for himself was keel boating on the Ohio and Mississippi rivers, carrying the products of the fire-clay industries of this section to western and southern markets, hence the name "Captain."

He soon became interested in the manufacture of fire-brick, and in 1859 became part owner of a fleet of keel boats, and as his business increased, the keel boats were replaced by tow boats, several of which he owned and operated for a number of years.

Since 1881 Mr. Porter has devoted his entire attention to manufacturing. He is now sole owner of the Aetna, Eagle, and Union Fire-brick works of New Cumberland, and is also largely interested in the Sligo, Clifton, and Enterprise Brick Works, and the Black-Horse Sewer-Pipe and Terra Cotta works as well. Besides this, he is the principal owner of the Chelsea Iron Stone China and Decorated Ware works, which was recently constructed and cost more than $100,000.

One year ago, where this magnificent building now stands was a weed patch, and the rapidity with which this gigantic enterprise was completed and put into operation illustrates the energy with which Mr. Porter goes into any enterprise.

The entire building is constructed of fire-brick, over 1,500,000 having been used. For the foundation, 2,200 perches of stone were required. The lower walls are eighteen inches and the upper walls thirteen inches thick. Eight kilns sixteen and one-half feet in diameter and fifty feet high are completed. The power is furnished by a 130-horse power Corliss engine. The building contains eighteen different departments, in each of which different parts of the work is done. It covers a full acre of ground, contains 620 windows, and the ventilation is as nearly perfect as possible. Although the works have been in operation but a short time, they are turning out ware of a superior quality, and everything indicates a prosperous future for the Chelsea China Company.

Most men who succeed as well in business as Mr. Porter has done are somewhat too conscious of the fact, but he is as modest and unassuming as he is energetic and successful, and the greater part of the facts is this sketch were obtained from his neighbors and friends. The following from the Hancock County Independent (paper) show the estimation in which he is held by those who know him best, and proves also that he is ever ready to do what he can for the good of his country: "The citizens of New Cumberland and the manufacturers along the river are indebted to John Porter more than anyone else for the completion of the railroad to this place.

His untiring energy and push have secured for the people the services of a road that would not have been built, to the least, by Mr. Porter, having determined to get the road, never looked back, and the New Cumberland branch is here today, a monument to his enterprise, perseverance, and untiring energy. New Cumberland has reason to be proud that she has such a man to lead her out of the wilderness."

The original Globe brickyard was started as Standard Fire Brick Company by a Pittsburgh company and erected by David Troup in 1874 and brother James Porter. In 1893, John Porter purchased some 35 acres of land outside of Newell, WV, known as Kenilworth and began building a new Globe plant.

Sometime around 1904-1906 a devastating fire hit the original Globe plant. Mr. Porter concentrated all his efforts on bringing the new Globe plant into operation. In 1909 was incorporated and began full production until 1970 when the facility was purchased and merged with Combustion Engineering of Stamford, CN, and became known as Globe Refractories, Inc.

In an interview with William Porter, grandson of John Porter, who in 1976 was president of Globe Refractories, stated that despite being acquired by a large company, they still treat Globe like the original board of directors did. He said that you still have to justify economically any capital expenditure, and they haven't been turned down yet. He also stated that we began working for the company in 1934 as a laborer, and getting paid 45¢ an hour and no fringes. Average hourly rate in 1976 was close to $5.00 an hour with benefits.[2]

End of Article

Obituary Captain John Porter[3]

Death Claims Captain Porter, Paving Brick Plant Founder
Pioneer in Industry, Riverman, and Legislator
Born in Ohio
Funeral Thursday Afternoon from Home in Kenilworth.

*F*uneral services for the late Captain John Porter, 83, oldest brick manufacturer in the United States, former riverman, and ex-sheriff of Hancock County, WV, who died at his home in Kenilworth, below Newell, at 5 o'clock last evening following two weeks' illness, will be conducted at the late residence at 1 o'clock Thursday afternoon. Rev. H. M. Hosack, pastor of the Newell Presbyterian Church, of which the deceased was a member, will officiate. Burial will be made in Riverview cemetery, East Liverpool.

Captain Porter has the distinction of making the first paving brick ever made in this section. In the late "eighties," he engaged in the business near New Cumberland, when he organized the Globe Brick Company. In 1893 he disposed of this plant and erected a factory at Kenilworth, of which company he was president at the time of his death. When Mr. Porter first began the manufacturing business, he and his helpers made brick by hand, turning out 3,500 bricks a day and firing about two kilns a week. Today the firm is producing 100,000 bricks per day and fires several kilns weekly.

Captain Porter's name was on the first paving brick laid in the city of Steubenville, Ohio, on a section of Third Street in 1884. In 1910, twenty-six years later, officials at Steubenville wrote Mr. Porter that not one dollar had been spent in repairs to this section of the street since it was laid, excepting when the street was torn up to construct street car lines and lay water mains.

Mr. Porter also supplied street paving brick to Cleveland, Columbus, Springfield, Cincinnati, Bellaire, Newark, Dayton, and East Liverpool through 1885. Vitrified brick was shipped from the Porter plant to the iron mills at Pittsburgh before the days of the railroad on the West Virginia side of the river. The brick was loaded in boats, with horses used to tow them. In the same manner, wood was shipped to the brick plant to be used in firing the kilns.

In early life, Captain Porter operated a line of steamboats and barges on the Ohio and Mississippi Rivers between Pittsburgh and New Orleans. He was the owner of the steamboat which bore his name that made the meteoric cruise up the Ohio River from Memphis in 1877 with several members of the crew suffering from yellow fever. All along the river, attempts were made to land the sick so that they could secure medical care, but everywhere crowds of people flocked to the wharves, armed with shotguns and prevented the infected craft from making a landing.

Late summer the boat stopped on the Ohio side of the river near Gallipolis[4], where the ill-fated voyage had its ending. Here the disease raged all winter, six persons dying from its effect.

Captain Porter was born in Martins Ferry, Ohio, August 7, 1838, being a son of Moses Porter and Eliza Spratt Porter. He was united in marriage to Miss Carrie Mahan of Arroyo, WV, December 7, 1870, with whom he had four sons and one daughter; Fred G., J. Bennett, J. Nessly and Sydney C. Porter. Mrs. Fred B. Lawrence, survive. There are also 13 grandchildren. Mr. and Mrs. Porter celebrated their golden wedding anniversary a little over a year ago.

In politics Mr. Porter was a staunch Republican. He was sheriff of Hancock County for one term from 1891-1895. He was also a member of the upper branch of the legislature, being elected to two terms, with the first being in 1911. His son, J. Ness Porter, is now a member of the West Virginia senate.

Family Links:
Parents:
Moses Porter (1808-1845)
Eliza Spratt Porter (1814-1899)

Spouse:
Carrie A. Mahan Porter (1845-1927)

Children:
John Chester Porter (1870-1875)
William Keefer Porter (1872-1886)
Frederick Gregg Porter (1878-1933)
J. Nessly Porter (1885-1933)

Siblings:
William Porter (1840-1870)
James Porter (1843-1910)*
Josephine Porter (1844-1857)

* *James Porter was the father to Mary Elizabeth Porter from New Cumberland. Mary was born March 2, 1910, and died August 2, 2007. Captain John Porter was her uncle.*

Photo of Captain John Porter
Photo courtesy of Brick, Volume 29, page 389

End Obituary Article

Endnotes

A Special Dedication
Mr. Walter "Peanuts" Czernecki

1. Information recorded from Mr. John Kuzio, October 2016 by the writer.
2. Death Certificates obtained from on-line Find-a-Grave of New Cumberland Cemetery for Walter and Daughter Walena. The certificate for son Domineck is misrepresented on the site and could not be included.

Introduction
Growing up in New Cumberland

1. Clinker – a clinker is a mass of hard, fused rock that is formed from coal burning too hot. Instead of ash forming as the coal is burned, the coal burns so hot that it fuses itself together. This hard mass would lodge between the grate openings and prevent the grates from moving. In most cases the clinker would have to be hammered out to the free the grate. – *en.wikipedia.org/clinker*

Chapter One
Brickmaking in New Cumberland

1. *History of the Clay-Working Industry in the United States*, (Ref. 53, page 209).
2. United States Geological Survey, Bulletin No. 279, *Kittanning and Rural Valley Quadrangles, Pennsylvania*, by Charles Butts, 1906 Government Printing Office, page 163, 164, 167.
3. United States Geological Survey, White, I. C., *Stratigraphy of bituminous coal and clay fields of Pennsylvania, Ohio, and West Virginia*. Bulletin 65, page 212.
4. Sanborn Insurance Map Company, 1897, Library of Congress

Chapter Two
Location of Rockyside

1. Map of Ohio, Brooke, Hancock Counties, West Virginia Geological Survey, 1924, I. C. White State Geologist – Map courtesy of Dan Tassey – Hancock County Assessor's Office

2. *West Virginia Department of Highways*, Joseph Juszczak, Division Six Assistant District Engineer – Construction

3. *Official Transportation Map of West Virginia*, 1936, State of West Virginia – Map courtesy of Dan Tassey – Assessors Office

Chapter Three
Rockyside a Forgotten Community

1. Ms. Alice Cooper was first mentioned by my father in a DVD video he made in April 1994. Ms. Cooper was later validated by my cousin Gertrude Ludovici whose mother gave her the middle name of Alice, after the schoolteacher. Researching the last name came up with no results. Even changing the last name from a (C) to a (K) showed no results. I know her first name was Alice, but no information regarding the last name could be found.

2. Mr. Tony LaNeve, out of 14 children was third to be born and the oldest son, resided in Newell, WV. His father, Ralph came from Italy around 1914. Tony taught school for many years and enlisted to fight in the war along with his brother Al. He returned in 1945 and taught school in Chester. Information obtained from brother Ed from East Liverpool, OH, September 2016. Grandfather to Vince LaNeve from Chester.

3. Ms. Eleanor M. (Burskey) Kobily from New Cumberland taught school around 1924-30. She would have been 15 years old.

Chapter Four
Clay Mining in Hancock County, WV

1. *History of the Panhandle; Being historical collections of the counties of Ohio, Brooke, Marshall and Hancock, W.Va.* – Compiled and written by J. H. Newton, G. G. Nichols and A. G. Sprankle – Wheeling, W.Va. – Published by J. A. Caldwell 1879.

Chapter Four - Continued

2. www.sciencelearn.org - Definition of Clay
3. *Brick & Clay Record* – Volume 32-33, page 60
4. *Encyclopedia of Civil Engineering, Historical, Theoretical, and Practice* by Edward Cresy, Chapter II, page 661
5. *Brick & Clay Record* – Volume 60, pages 464 & 465
6. *West Virginia Geological Survey*, Volume II, page 382-384
7. *West Virginia Geological Survey*, Volume II, page 381
8. *Clay Industry of the Panhandle Area*, page 284
9. *West Virginia Miners Health Safety & Training* – 1923, Document Nos. 904210.02/03

Chapter Five
Brickmaking South of New Cumberland

1. *The Brickmaker* – Vol. 17-20 – page 27
2. *History of New Cumberland, WV, Centennial Celebration – 1839 - 1939*

Chapter Six
Brickmaking North of New Cumberland

1. *History of the Panhandle; Being historical collections of the counties of Ohio, Brooke, Marshall and Hancock, W.Va.* – Compiled and written by J. H. Newton, G. G. Nichols and A. G. Sprankle – Wheeling, W.Va. – Published by J. A. Caldwell 1879.
2. *History of Hancock County, Virginia & West Virginia* – Jack Welch, Wheeling News, Printing & Litho Co. 1963 – digital version
3. See description in glossary section
4. Mack Manufacturing Company – Paving Brick & Blocks

Chapter Seven
The First Catholic Church & School in New Cumberland

1. Photo courtesy of David and Bonnie Burskey
2. Information courtesy of Mr. Jon-Erik Gilot, MLIS, Director of Archives & Records, Dioceses of Wheeling-Charleston.

Chapter Eight
Other Manufacturing in New Cumberland

Chelsea China Company
1. Information found on-line laurelhollowpark.net/Chelsea China
2. Photo courtesy of Hancock County Courier – Tina Tate

Cutler Steel/Duraloy Company
1 *History of the Duraloy Company* written by Thomas Rhett Heyward, Jr., covering a period from 1921 to 1953. Information provided by Current President of Duraloy Mr. Vince Schiavoni.
2 Picture compliments of Duraloy President Vince Schiavoni.

New Cumberland Glass Works
1. West Virginia Division of Culture & History

Hancock County Manufacturing
1. Hancock County Courier – Sesquicentennial Celebration 1839-1989
2. Ohio Valley Manufacturer, Wheeling, WV, May 23, 1907, page 20

Chapter Nine
The Zumer and the Zielinsky Families

1. *Encyclopedia Britannica.com*
2. *Goggle maps at goggle.com*

Chapter Ten
A Tribute to Captain John S. Porter "Brick King"

1. "History of the Upper Ohio Valley," Volume 1. Brant & Fuller, 1890
2. Interview of William Porter by Thomas Hess on November 22, 1976. Youngstown State University, Oral History Program, Brick Industry, History of Globe Refractories, Inc., O. H. 504
3. Obituary: East Liverpool Evening Review, East Liverpool, Columbiana County, OH. Wednesday, 08 Feb 1922, page 1.
4. Gallipolis, Ohio – On the Ohio River about mid-point between Huntington and Parkersburg, WV.

Photo Section
Photos for each Chapter

This section of the book is very special because as the old saying goes, "a picture is worth a thousand words." It is within this section I wanted to include as many pictures as were appropriate, so the reader has a true realization of what these brickyards, and especially Rockyside, looked like. Unfortunately, actual pictures of Rockyside, as it appeared in late 1800 or early 1900, do not exist. Some pictures were taken while photographing the brickyards that showed what some of the actual homes looked like on the hillside. Several pictures of the smaller houses (almost like shacks) were obtained from friends and relatives and will also be included. These close-ups of the buildings will give you an understanding of how they were constructed. There were no pictures taken on Rockyside that would show how the actual homes were situated.

The quality of some of these photos is poor at best. It is really hard to see detail, especially when trying to increase their size. The mine maps are also difficult to view because of the "blue" paper they were printed on. Therefore, I've elected to show more of a distance image than a close up. I do show close ups of portions of buildings instead of the entire building. I will hopefully make this clear as I identify each picture.

I've tried to include as many important photos as possible to enhance the overall quality of the book from a reading perspective. I want the reader, after reading this book, to be left with a practical impression of what Rockyside once looked like. The reader should keep in mind that photos were rarely taken because owning a camera and processing film was a luxury. However, I have been extremely fortunate to receive the photos I did so I could share the experience.

Photos are identified and arranged by actual book chapter. These additional photos will help provide additional detail and in some cases additional reading.

A Special Dedication
Mr. Walter "Peanuts" Czernecki

Death Certificate of Walter Czernecki

Death Certificate of Walena Czernecki
Information courtesy of Find-a-Grave, New Cumberland Cemetery

Information regarding son Domineck was not available.

A Special Recognition and Tribute
Mr. John J. Kuzio

This section would not be complete without the special piece of onionskin paper that John Kuzio gave me on our first meeting. This onionskin paper is what started us on our journey. The paper measures 23 ½ " by 16 ¾ " and is cut irregularly at the top and bottom. It is how John remembered the location of brickyards, family homes, clay tipples, coal tipples, and all the rest. Locations were a little off, but the paper contained enough to start piecing the parts together.

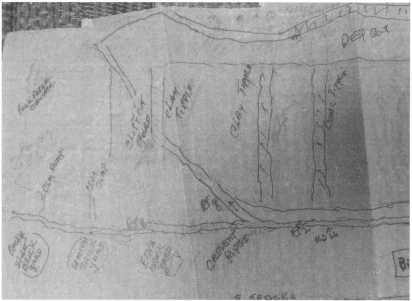

Photo of left side of the onionskin paper

Thank you again John Kuzio for allowing me to own this remarkable piece of history. I'm going to make sure I don't lose it, so I'm going to give it to George Hines to place in the New Cumberland City Building for safe keeping and for everyone to see.

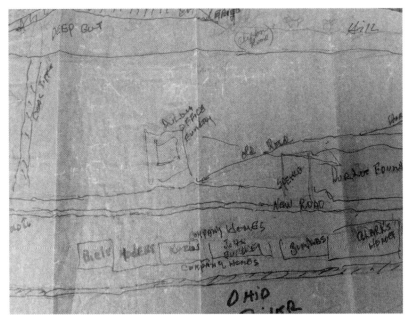

Photo of middle section of onionskin paper

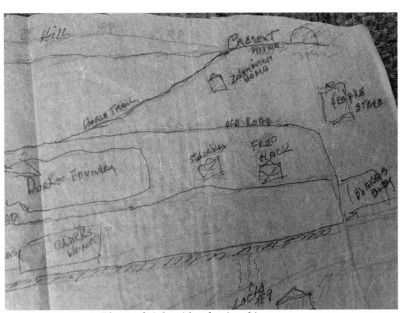

Photo of right side of onionskin paper
Photos courtesy of T. W. Zielinsky

Chapter One
Brickmaking in New Cumberland

The first set of maps I obtained from the Sanborn Insurance Company was dated 1890. On the left is Lone Star Fire Brick Works located just north of the mouth of Kings Creek situated on the Ohio River. Next, on the right are the Sligo and the Anderson Brothers Brickyards working your way north toward New Cumberland.

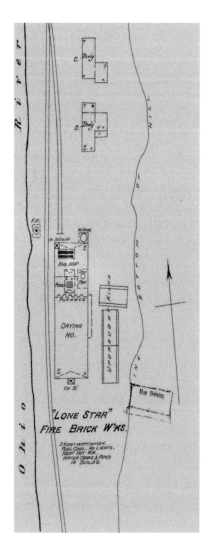

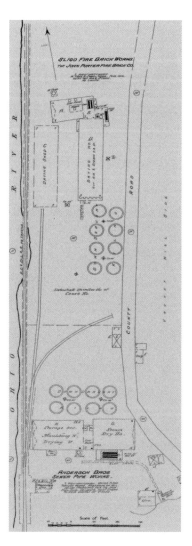

The next series of brickyards, continuing north toward New Cumberland, will be the American Fire Brick Works, and then the Freeman & Company Fire Brick Works. Freeman was the first brickyard established near the mouth of Holberts Run.

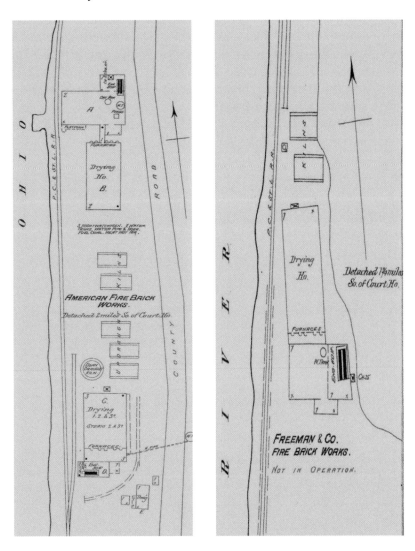

These brickyards extending from the mouth of Kings Creek northward into New Cumberland were first established in 1834. In 1890, the Sanborn Insurance Company began recognizing and detailing them in map form.

The next brickyard and sewer pipe company was known as the Black-Horse Works, located just south of the S curve along the river just outside of New Cumberland. This was a fairly large facility that also included a ferry. You can see it highlighted on the left in the Ohio River.

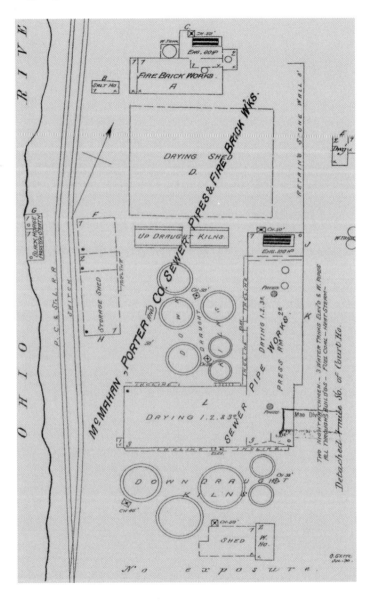

Before moving to the northern part of New Cumberland, I need to show the Chelsea China Company and the New Cumberland Glass Works as they existed in 1890. As indicated on the diagram, the glass works was still under construction. This glass facility was located on South Chester Street about in the middle between Morris and Troy Streets.

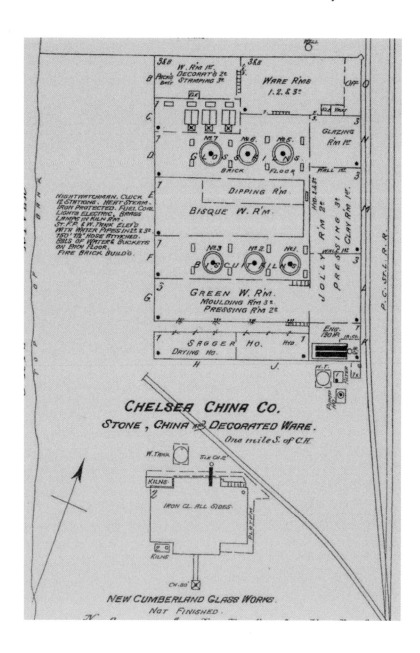

Proceeding north just past the intersection of Routes 2 and 8 would start the Clifton Works. Just slightly south of the intersection was the Mack Manufacturing Office building.

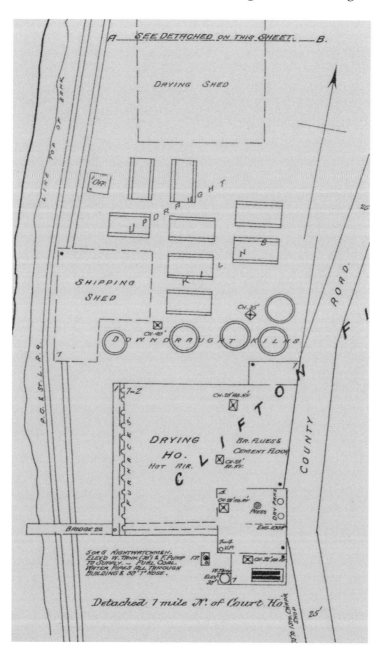

Continuing north from Clifton is the Upper Clifton Works, which will eventually become the Crescent Brickyard.

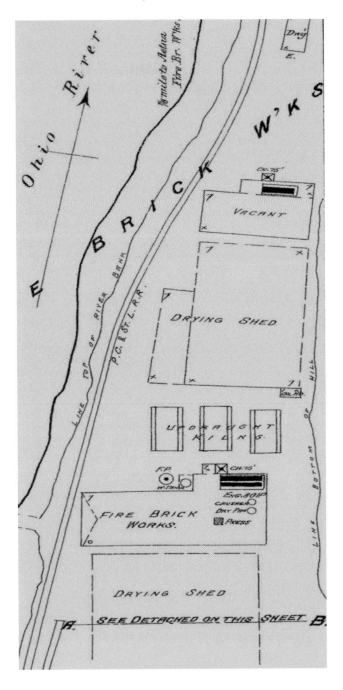

Next in line continuing north is the Etna, or in 1890, the Aetna Fire Brick Works.

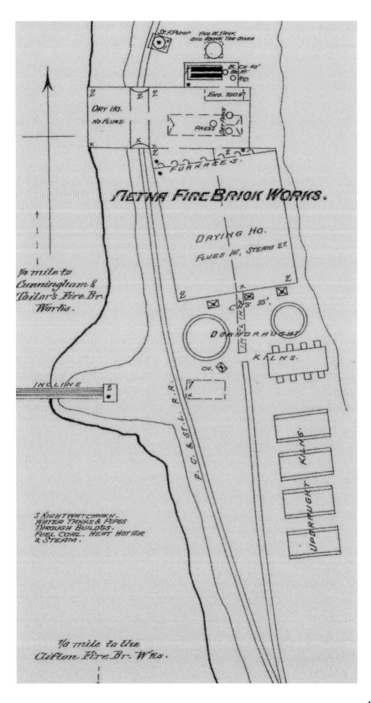

Next was the Cunningham and Taylor Fire Brick Works that apparently didn't last long. After a disastrous fire, it was never rebuilt. Just to the north of Cunningham, the Eagle Fire Brick Works was established and later converted into making sewer pipe. *(Picture became distorted while trying to increase its size)*

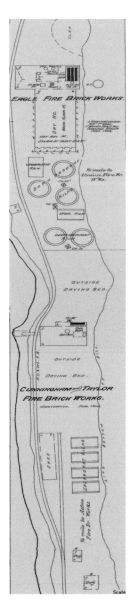

Just north of the Eagle plant was the Union Fire Brick Works. Remnants of this plant still exist today with the main clay crusher building still standing. This building was important in determining distances to find where the other plants were located across this property. A quarter mile north of the Union plant is the Rockyside Fire Brick Works. Rockyside wouldn't show up on land maps until 1897, even though the plant was started in 1870. Three-quarters of a mile farther north from the Union plant was the first Globe Fire Brick Works.

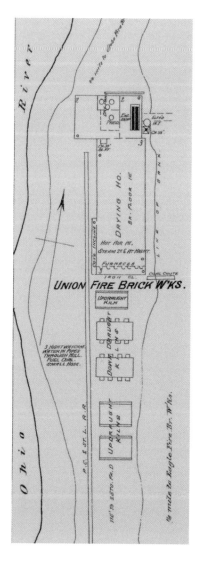

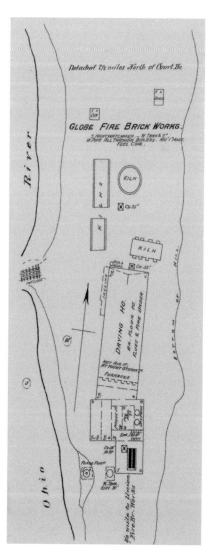

Chapter Two
Location of Rockyside

Rockyside is located one-mile north out of New Cumberland on either side of Route 2. Rockyside is the hilltop area as shown in the photo. It extends from near the bottom of Deep Gut Run to the John D. Rockefeller Center. The entire hillside on both sides of the road is considered Rockyside.

Photo courtesy of Greg Blake New Cumberland

This photo appears to have been taken in the winter. In the distance (top of circle), the Rockefeller Center is visible under magnification; however, the bus garage built by the school system hadn't been started, so it's unclear what year this photo was taken.

Route 2 is the black line in the center, while old Route 66 is the white line on the left side of the circle. Directly below the 66 numbers, next to the river, is a dark area. This area is what is left of the Union Brickyard. Where the New

Cumberland Dam ties to the West Virginia shoreline is where the Rockyside Brickyard was located, and north from there one-half mile, the first Globe Brickyard.

Before 1958, you were required to travel on old Route 66 to get up to and past Rockyside. In order to do that, you needed to take Route 2 (now Route 8) out of New Cumberland toward New Manchester (formerly Pughtown). You would drive up the hill about one-half mile and turn left down a fairly steep road called Clifton Hill Road. You would drive down and across a small bridge, and then start up the road and around the hillside overlooking the brickyards.

Photo of old Route 66 coming off of Clifton Hill road proceeding up and around the hillside past the brickyards. Mule stable is in the foreground. Upper top corner is clay car transfer shed. Clay from the Etna mine is pulled up and around the bend to the clay tipples on the other side of the hill.
Photo courtesy of Mack Manufacturing Company

The following map clearly indicates the location of Rockyside, which is on the hillside just north of Deep Gut Run. Shown on the map are a church and a school. The gray line running zigzag across the page to Ferndale School is actually Rockyside Road.

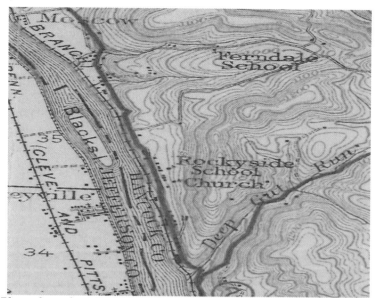

Photo shows location of Ferndale School, Rockyside Church and School
Map courtesy of West Virginia Geological Survey 1924

A view of old Route 66 looking south. To the right side, over the hill would
be where the Union Brickyard was located
Photo courtesy of T. W. Zielinsky

Chapter Three
Rockyside a Forgotten Community

The following photos are a collection of what homes looked like when nearly fourteen families lived on Rockyside. This picture (date unknown) is of old Route 66 heading north. The house on the right in the background is one variety of home built in this area by the Mack Company.

Old Route 66 coming from New Cumberland driving north
Photo courtesy of James and Bernadette Zucosky

Just north of the previous picture is this smaller house (almost shack like) located on the left side of old Route 66 near or slightly past the Etna clay dump. The house by 1949 was abandoned.

Photo of Alex Zucosky foreground with his wife Josephine and Nellie Burskey (wife of Joseph Martin Burskey) taken in 1949
Photo courtesy of James and Bernadette Zucosky

We were able to identify some fourteen families living in either single dwelling or duplex style homes, where two families shared one house. Information from all of our sources indicates that only one large wooden house was built on Rockyside. This home was located slightly south of where the current West Virginia State Police barracks is located. While researching the hillside, George Hines made a keen observation that has served as our primary reference point. Approximately three-tenths of a mile south of Rockyside Road stands a 20-foot tall holly tree. This happens to be the only holly tree on the entire Rockyside hillside.

126

Holly tree approximately 0.3 miles south of Rockyside road
Photo courtesy of T. W. Zielinsky

Directly behind this tree are the remains of the one-room schoolhouse and just about 50-yards farther south, along the same line, is the location of where the Catholic Church was built.

Remains of the one-room schoolhouse taken from the front
Photo by T. W. Zielinsky

Standing inside of the school, photo of right front corner
Photo courtesy of T. W. Zielinsky

Unfortunately, there were no pictures of the actual school building, but George Hines and I did find what remains of the school walls. The above photo is the right corner of the building taken from inside. The next photo is the same corner showing a doorway into the building, taken from the outside.

Photo remains of Rockyside Schoolhouse entrance
Photo courtesy of T. W. Zielinsky

The walls are built with double rows of brick, and this right corner section measures about four feet high.

Photo standing at the front of building showing right front corner and partial front wall in the leafs – Photo courtesy of T. W. Zielinsky

Our research turned up three teachers who taught in this school; a Miss Alice Cooper, a Mr. Tony LaNeve, and a Miss Eleanor Burskey. No information can be found on Alice Cooper or whether the spelling of her last name is correct. Her first name was Alice because my cousin Gertrude Ludovici's middle name is Alice, named after this schoolteacher who was best friends with her mother Josephine (Zumer) Reese.

Mr. Tony LaNeve's father, Ralph, came from Italy and settled in Newell, WV. Ralph was the youngest of seven LaNeve brothers. Tony was the third child born of fourteen children (nine boys and five girls) and the oldest boy in the family, while brother Ed is the youngest.

Mr. Tony LaNeve is the grandfather of Vince LaNeve from Chester, WV, and brother to Ed LaNeve from East Liverpool, OH. Vince's father is Ronald LaNeve, not to be confused with his great uncle, also Ronald.

129

Photo of the five of the seven LaNeve brothers – Ralph LaNeve, father of 14 including Tony the third oldest and Ed LaNeve the youngest – Photo reprinted with permission courtesy of Mr. Ed LaNeve

Miss Eleanor Burskey, from New Cumberland, taught on this hillside, but no one is sure exactly what years she taught. She was born in 1910. This next photo is a picture dated 1924-30 Rockyside School. Miss Burskey is pictured with these students. The information I received indicated she was the teacher. That would make her 14 or 15 when this photo was taken.

There is little detail in the picture with the exception of the students. The land and area around the students is hilly and quite barren with only a few bushes to the left and behind the students. The white behind the students appears to be coming from the brickyard and must be smoke from the kilns.

As you will see by the names of the students, some children are from families identified as living on Rockyside hillside, while other children would be from either the north end of New Cumberland or from the homes in and close to Deep Gut Run and Etna Hollow areas. Notice as well the spelling of the last names. These would eventually be shortened or changed altogether. As an example; Alex Zukowski's name would become just Zucosky.

130

Photo of Rockyside School Children 1924-30
Photo courtesy of Dave and Bonnie Burskey

1st Row – Ray Powers, J. Narcavish, Paul Sweat, Earl Hoffman, James Sweat, Frank Salisberry, Clarence Reese, Charles Barton, Alex Zukowski, Marion Graham
2nd Row – Delpha Barton, Mildred Barton, Irene Parker, Genevieve Zubreska, Helen Bagenski, Arles Hoffman, Cecil Parker, Marvin Sweat
3rd Row – Mildred Hoffman, Ethel Angus, Mildred Graham, Robert Graham, Eleanor Burskey – teacher, Edward Sweat, Helen Graham, Helen Sweat, Lenora Powers, Saraha Reese.

The next photo was unique as well as it represents the 4H club on Rockyside. This community took into consideration just about everything one would need. I remember my father explaining that after the Catholic school was opened in 1920, he had to leave a perfectly good school on Rockyside and walk over a mile to attend Catholic school. He also remembered Alice Cooper as his teacher, so she must have taught sometime before 1920.

131

Photo of Rockyside 4H Club – date unknown
Photo courtesy of Dave and Bonnie Burskey

This undated photo shows a slightly older Miss Burskey and three members of the 4H Club. The three girls are from left to right: Vida, Anna (behind Miss Burskey), and Georgia. With little explanation who these girls might be, Anna, standing behind Eleanor, might be her older sister. Anna Burskey would marry John Roefaro and would have a son and daughter. The daughter would be Eleanor (Roefaro) Straight, former Hancock County Clerk who passed away on November 7, 2016. *Small world indeed.*

Miss Burskey would eventually marry Ted Kobily, move into New Cumberland, and continue teaching. She died in 1990.

132

As the reader can see by the photos, there really isn't much left on or along Rockyside hillside. There are several larger sections of walls in between the area of Route 2 and Route 66 that are buried under tons of dirt and debris that followed the construction of the new Route 2.

Numerous trips across this densely wooded and briar filled land, from the road to the top of hill, did not reveal any further evidence of dwellings except for the church. The impression of where the church was built is quite evident. It is hard to decipher the impression in these photos, but brick, roof slate, and broken glass are scattered where the church once stood. Even the sewer pipe used as a foundation is still in place.

Church location standing left front corner shooting toward hillside
Photo courtesy of T. W. Zielinsky

The above photo is where the church once stood. Time and Mother Nature had their way and altered much of this particular spot. It is hard to distinguish what George and I actually saw, and this is after about 30 minutes of stomping the briars and branches down.

This next photo shows some sewer pipe still left in the ground at the corners and along the sides of the church where the foundation should have been. Since permission to build this church was given in September 1904, and the church was built and dedicated on December 24, 1904, it had to be built rather quickly. According to John Kuzio, foundations at that time were dug by hand; then sewer pipe was inserted into the ground and filled with brick and dirt. Railroad ties were then used to build the cross supports, and the building followed.

Sewer pipe, brick and slate found at the church site
Photo courtesy of T. W. Zielinsky

Bricks used for this and all construction on Rockyside were made from the Mack Manufacturing brickworks. This specially made building brick was ingenious in design. As you can see from the next set of photos, there were two oval shaped risers built into the brick. Along the bottom and the two sides were grooves hollowed into the brick. This allowed the brick to be used in an interlocking, crisscrossed fashion for increased stability and strength. Also, one edge of the brick was beveled at a slight angle. This allowed the brick to also be used for road paving and allowed horses' hooves to walk on the brick

134

without fear of stumbling.   Each brick weighed in at nearly ten pounds.

Pictures and the story behind the first Catholic Church will be found in the Photo Section under Chapter Seven.

Building Brick by Mack Manufacturing front side
Photo courtesy of T. W. Zielinsky

Building Brick by Mack Manufacturing back side
Photo courtesy of T. W. Zielinsky

Mack Manufacturing Brick Logo
Photo courtesy of Mack Manufacturing

The Mack Company built all the houses on the hillside for married couples. They were built as duplex type structures, each having four rooms per side, two on the top floor and two on the bottom floor, with a coal/wood shed in between the structures. Bedrooms were on the top floor with the kitchen in the bottom. Two fireplaces were located in the house, one on the top floor and one on the bottom floor. The top floor fireplace provided heat for sleeping, and the bottom floor fireplace provided not only heat, but was also used for cooking meals. The kitchen contained a smaller fireplace, while a larger fireplace was located on the top level and was shared between the two upper rooms.

Single men had to stay in the barracks building. One building was used for sleeping, and the other used for taking their meals. The original barracks was built entirely from wood and was destroyed by fire around 1920. A brick building was constructed away from the original barracks and thought to be near the church. An exhaustive search for the barracks did not reveal its location. It must be assumed that the barracks was somewhere in line with where Route 2 was constructed, and any remains were plowed under.

Photo shows three houses: two duplexes center & left, and one single-family house on the right – all shown under arrows – Photo courtesy of Mack Manufacturing

The house to the right directly behind the chimney was identified as the Zumer home. John Kuzio distinctly remembered climbing up the hill to serve mass. He would stop

136

at the Zumer home, cross the road, and climb yet another hill to get to the church. He stated this was the only large wooden framed single family home on the left side of old Route 66. It was larger than the other single-family homes.

In the next photo, if you look really closely, behind the house there is a faint image of the steeple to the church, arrow on the right side of photo. I passed this photo to Helen Brancazio, and she clearly remembers this home and dancing on the porch on Saturday nights.

Photo of Zumer home - image of church steeple on the upper right side
Photo courtesy of Mack Manufacturing

Photo shows a close up of the middle duplex house from the previous photo
Photo courtesy of Mack Manufacturing

Photo of Zumer house foundation found in 2016 taken from roadway
Photo courtesy of T. W. Zielinsky

This foundation can be seen in the black and white photo directly to the right and under the porch. The finding of this foundation and the proximity to the Union brickyard enabled the writers the ability to locate the church. This foundation rests approximately one-half mile from Rockyside Road walking south on old Route 66.

Once we found the foundation, we reversed our steps and walked one-half mile from Rockyside Road heading south along Route 2. We then cut up over the hillside while continuing to walk south toward New Cumberland until we came upon the hillside imprint of the church foundation.

The next two photos are the foundation from below the hillside (the porch would have been located to the left of this part of the foundation) and part of the right back wall with the fireplace. This last photo would be in the lowest section of the house.

Photo of foundation of the Zumer house taken from below hillside
Photo courtesy of T. W. Zielinsky

Foundation and brick wall with fireplace at the site of the Zumer home located along old Route 66. This house sat on the left side of the hill going north on Route 66.

Part of the back wall and fireplace of the Zumer house
Photo courtesy of T. W. Zielinsky

Left photo of Chet and Alex Spilecki on pony with sister Helen (Spilecki) Brancazio standing with the white dress – Right photo of Chet and Doris Spilecki with her dolly - Photos courtesy of Wanda Spilecki

Notice this brick duplex house and in the background a storage shed for coal or wood. Buildings did not have bathroom facilities. Family members would use chamber pots and then empty them into the outdoor facilities. There were several large two sided outdoor facilities to accommodate the people on Rockyside.

In the photo on the right, you can see how the bricks were laid in a crisscross pattern. You can see that brick was first laid in horizontal courses, about three high, and then every third-row of brick runs crossways using those joints for added integrity.

In the next photo, the foreground is just plain dirt with only a few weeds growing alongside the house. The entire Rockyside hillside was exactly the same, just dirt and weeds.

Photo – Back is Ed Reese and Emily Stolarczyk
Robert (Dink) Reese in the front – date taken unknown
Photo courtesy of Ed and Patty Reese

One house existed on Rockyside that contained seven rooms on one side and five rooms on the other. Built as an oversized duplex, it was built out of wood and brick. Two fairly large families lived here; Zielinsky on one side, Zucosky on the other. Another structure was located to the right of the building, but the photo is too grainy to determine what type of structure it is. Some believe it was an outdoor facility and then another brick duplex to the right of that structure.

On the left side there is a gray shadow being blocked under a cloud of smoke which makes it appear that another building is under construction. This building would soon be home to the Stolarczyk family.

Photo of brick and wooden houses – notice three chimneys' instead of the usual two meaning an exceptionally large house –
Photo courtesy of Mack Manufacturing

This next photo, taken a few years later, shows additionally completed buildings along the hillside.

Photo indicates that homes were completed and more were added – date unknown - Photo courtesy of Mack Manufacturing

Homes were built with the same general brick style all through this area including the Deep Gut Run area. The next photo is the Glover house, built near the site of the existing Water Treatment plant. The white area in the background is part of the rail system taking clay from the Etna Mine around the hill to the clay tipples.

Photo Charlotte and Ellis Glover in the back, Lloyd and Owen Glover with Kenny Reese standing in front of Ellis, and Butch and Bobby Reese, Clara and Buzzy Shepard in front – Photo courtesy of Ed and Patty Reese

The reason more foundations were not found is that during the construction of the new Route 2, sections of road were probably built over much of what remained on the hillside after these families moved into New Cumberland. The writer did find large sections of bricks and slate in the area between old Route 66 and Route 2, but nothing found could be identified as to what type of structure these might have belonged to.

A couple of large circular brick sections were found that would give indication these were the remains of a water well, or as they were called back then, "spring houses." A number of large wooden beams were also located in this same area, but in a very decayed state. These beams would indicate either foundational supports or sections from a roof.

The other buildings not found were the outside bathrooms or "outhouses." According to our sources, there were several large buildings capable of handling six people at one time. One building was just across the road from the

Union plant. Sections of brick were found in this location, but we cannot be certain what they came from.

Photo of a section of circular brick
Photo courtesy of T. W. Zielinsky

Photo of a large section of wall
These photos taken in the area between Route 2 and old Route 66
Photo courtesy of T. W. Zielinsky

Chapter Four
Clay Mining in Hancock County, WV

Clay mining started in 1830 near the mouth of Holberts Run, and the clay was shipped by barge to Pittsburgh where it was then made into bricks for the steel industry. A couple of young entrepreneurs decided to start making brick in West Virginia, and the rest is history.

Those early clay mines south of New Cumberland have been sealed. The last mine to be sealed was the Chapman or Acme Mine, as it was sometimes called, just south of New Cumberland at the bottom of Ballantyne Road. The sealing of this last mine did not happen without incident. The mine supplied clay for the West Virginia Fire Clay Company, and when it was abandoned, it was not completely sealed. Some young boys decided to crawl inside to explore and got lost. It took rescue crews several hours to find the boys, and then the entrance was permanently closed.

Photo of the closed-off entrance to the Chapman or Acme Mine
Photo courtesy of T. W. Zielinsky

The challenge for the writers was to try and find the exact location of clay mines that existed when the brickyards were operating. Our contacts had difficulty remembering

145

where the mine entrances were, but knew they were located very near to the brickyards they served.

I was blessed to have found Joe Juszczak from the West Virginia Department of Highways who not only owned the existing brickyard property but also had the original mine maps for the brickyards. The next photo is from the upper part of the map, which states: *Map of Mack Mfg. Co. Mines, W. VA. Dated June 25, 1923.* This map is 31 inches wide by 68 ½ inches long or (2.5 feet by 5.7 feet). It shows exactly were all mine entrances were located.

Photo of logo on original mine map for Mack Manufacturing Company Dated June 25, 1923 – Photo courtesy of Joe Juszczak

The writers have identified locations to all mines listed on the mine map blueprint. A recap is as follows:

> Globe Mine – still exists and is partway open,
> Rockyside Mine – still exists and is partway open,
> Union Mine – completely sealed,
> Eagle Mine – completely sealed,
> Crescent Mine number one – completely sealed,
> Crescent Mine number two – completely sealed,
> Crescent Mine number three – completely sealed,
> Acme Mine number one – completely sealed,
> Acme Mine number two – completely sealed,
> Etna Mine number one – completely sealed,
> Etna Mine number two – completely open.

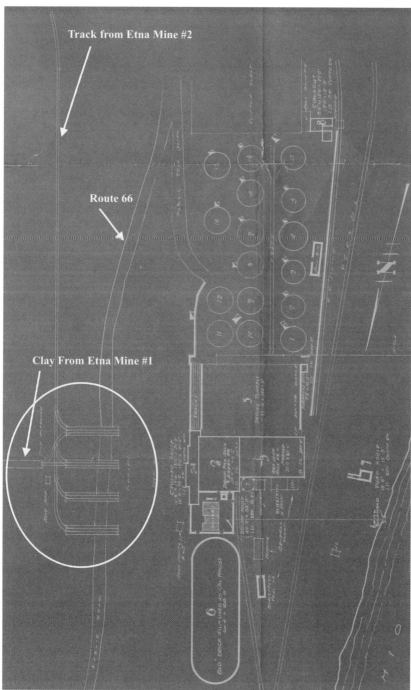

Photo of Crescent Brickyard – Etna Clay mine and tipples to the left with trail leading to the Etna Deep Gut Mine coming from the top left side

147

Photo of actual Mack Manufacturing Mine Map
Photo courtesy of Joe Juszczak and Newbrough Photo

148

The Mack Mine map was extremely valuable in identifying the total number of clay seams that were mined into the Rockyside hillside. The reader must be aware that most of these clay seams are coming up from the river into the hillside. Sitting on top the clay is coal, and sitting on top of the coal is roughly 30 or more feet of sandstone. Finally, several feet of earth and dirt cover over the sandstone.

The exact locations of the mines will not be included in this book; however, pictures for several mines will be shown. What is interesting to note is that while I was doing this research using the Mack map, I also found, through the West Virginia Department of Mines, mine maps for the Acme Mine and Crescent Mine number three on Hardins Run Road. Where the property lines leave off on the Mack map, they begin on the Acme map and continue onto the Crescent map. This means there was a continuous seam of Kittanning fire clay running from Globe all the way to Hardins Run. The seam does drop about 100 feet until it disappears after the mouth of Kings Creek.

The first map (on top) is of the Acme Fire Clay Mine along Commerce and Straight Streets in New Cumberland. There are still various brick structures located in this area including a large chimney. The entrance to the actual mine has been sealed. The mine seams run up the entire hillside and make their way near and possibly under the New Cumberland Cemetery.

The second map (bottom) is of the Crescent Fire Clay Mine number three along Hardins Run Road. A tipple and other structures are still there, but the entrance to the mine has been sealed. This map shows mine seams running up the hillside through the backside and possibly under the New Cumberland Cemetery.

Notice that the first map fits perfectly in the space of the second map. This means these clay seams were all interconnected.

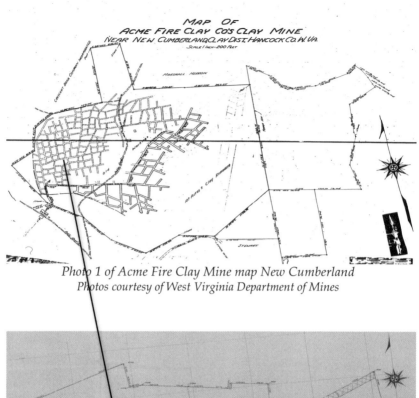

Photo 1 of Acme Fire Clay Mine map New Cumberland
Photos courtesy of West Virginia Department of Mines

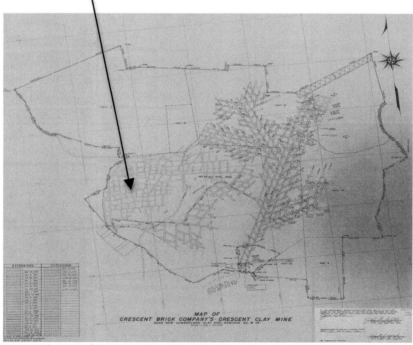

Photo 2 of Crescent Fire Clay Mine map on Hardins Run Road
Notice the top mines fit in the space on the left of the Crescent map

150

These photos show the mine seams for the Acme and the Crescent Clay mines and how they were closely aligned. Whether the owners knew this at the time is unknown.

Photo of Acme/Chapman Works on Commerce and Straight Streets as of 2016 - Photo courtesy of T. W. Zielinsky

Photo of Acme/Chapman Works as it appeared September 1946
Photo courtesy of George Hines

Notice the brick chimney located to the upper right of the photo.

Photo of Tipple at Crescent Clay Mine number three on Hardins Run Road
This was the last mine to close and be sealed in 1979
Photo courtesy of T. W. Zielinsky

Clay mines actually start in the northern part of Hancock County and run continuously through Hancock, Brooke, and Ohio counties. Some clay mines outside of Hancock County were never mined because of the difficulty of getting to the clay. However, coal, which lies on top of the clay, was easier to extract and a little more profitable.

152

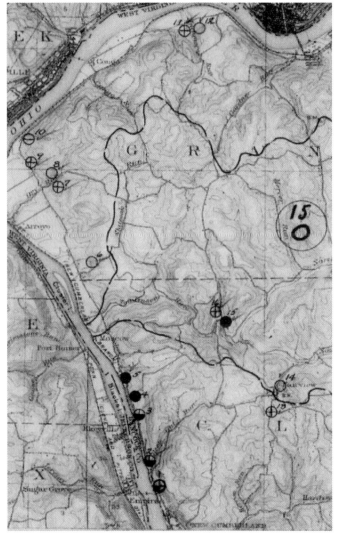

Photo of mines located from northern part of Chester to the Crescent Mine
two (circle with a cross) at the bottom of the map
Photo courtesy of West Virginia Department of Mines

This next map shows the mines located from Chelsea (New Cumberland) all the way into Brooke County. Notice circled in the center of the map the number of mines along Kings Creek and North Fork Road areas.

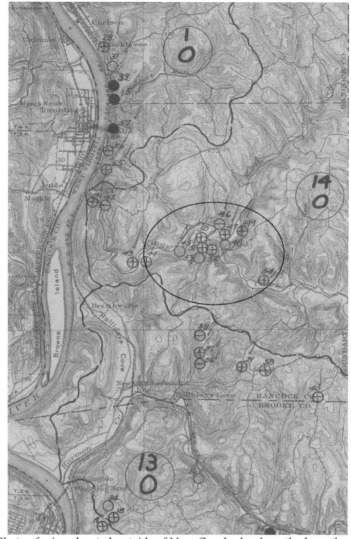

Photo of mines located outside of New Cumberland south along the
Ohio River toward Weirton
Photo courtesy of West Virginia Department of Mines

The following photos are from what is left of the Globe Mine north of New Cumberland and the Rockyside Mine, about in the same general location. They are partway open, and standing directly in front of the Globe mine entrance, you can feel a cool breeze blowing outward. When this photo was taken, the outside temperature was 85 degrees while the air temperature coming from the opening was probably 50 or cooler.

Photo of the remains of the Globe Mine north of New Cumberland
Photo courtesy of T. W. Zielinsky

Photo of the remains of the Rockyside Mine and part of a chimney in the foreground, south of the Globe Mine - Photo courtesy of T. W. Zielinsky

The Union and Eagle mines have been completely plowed over. Without specific map coordinates, no one would be able to locate these mines. Even with the proper map locations, one would have to use dynamite and heavy machinery to reopen the actual entrances.

The Etna mines are a little different. Etna Mine number one, which runs along Route 2, has been completely sealed. However, Etna Mine number two is completely open and could present a public hazard, so its exact location will not be reported in this book. Since the terrain has been drastically altered since 1904, it would be extremely difficult for anyone to actually find the Etna Mine.

Photo of Etna Mine from the ridge of the hillside
Photo courtesy of T. W. Zielinsky

It took almost an hour of climbing over extremely hazardous terrain just to determine whether we were in the right location of this mine, using only the information we had available at the time. Shale and other soft rocks made footing and standing extremely treacherous.

After we made our discovery and got some oxygen back into our lungs, we were able to take a few pictures. The amazingly fun part was the climb back down without killing ourselves, but we did make it safely.

156

Photo of Etna Mine close up – shows George Hines at the entrance
The opening is enormous - Photo courtesy of T. W. Zielinsky

Photo of the inside of the mine entrance, nearly completely filled with water
several feet deep from our observation - Photo courtesy of T. W. Zielinsky

Photo Crescent Clay Mine number two along North Chestnut Street
Photo courtesy of T. W. Zielinsky

The above photo is what is left of Crescent Clay Mine number two. The first mine was located near the intersection of Routes 2 and 8. This second entrance was located just off North Chestnut Street. In early 1900, this entrance was made off a side street called Chestnut Alley, which would be a short distance up the hillside. Not much remains with the exception of one telltale mark, copper-colored water that will never stop running.

All mines, once opened, will have the natural tendency to produce water, and this mine is no exception. Water has been seeping out of the ground since it was opened and will continue forever.

As you proceed north out of New Cumberland toward Rockyside, you will notice copper-colored water running off the hillside as you start up the hill. This is water coming from the first Etna Mine located about mid-range to the top of the hill. It too will continue to run forever.

In the following photo, you can see where the Crescent Mine number two entrance was approximately located. The street map clearly shows Chestnut Alley where the entrance was located, just 50-feet from North Chestnut and Fourth Street.

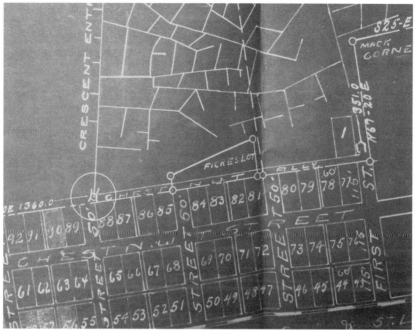

Photo of the Crescent Clay Mine number two (circle) located north along Chestnut Alley and directly off North Chestnut Street –the alley no longer exists – Photo courtesy of Joe Juszczak and T. W. Zielinsky

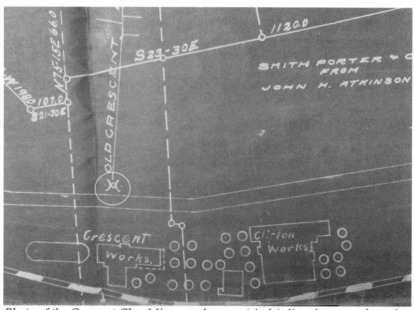

Photo of the Crescent Clay Mine number one (circle) directly across from the brickyard – Photo courtesy of Joe Juszczak and T. W. Zielinsky

159

Chapter Five
Brickmaking South of New Cumberland

Brickmaking and the production of sewer pipe initially started near the mouth of Holberts Run. Then starting south near the mouth of Kings Creek, plants were built north toward New Cumberland. These plants drew their clay from the hillside directly opposite of where the plant was built.

Plants that followed in order from the south, working north to New Cumberland were: Lone Star Brick Works, Sligo Brick and Sewer Pipe Works, Anderson Brothers Brick and Sewer Pipe Works, Claymont Brick Works, Freeman Brick Works, and finally the Black-Horse Brick and Sewer Pipe Works just outside of New Cumberland.

All of these plants were built initially with what machinery was available at that time (mid to late 1800). The Lone Star plant was the first to close while the others changed ownership a couple of times before also closing.

Photo Sligo Brick Works north of the mouth of Kings Creek
Photo courtesy of Mack Manufacturing

Photo Sligo Sewer Pipe Works north of the mouth of Kings Creek
Photo courtesy of Mack Manufacturing

No photos were found of the Lone Star plant, only a sketched image provided by the Sanborn Insurance Map Company.

Photo of Freeman's Landing Brick Works at the mouth of Holberts Run
Photo courtesy of Mack Manufacturing

Rare photo of the Claymont Brick and Sewer Pipe Works
Photo courtesy of Ohio Valley Manufacturer

This poor-quality photo of the Claymont Brick and Sewer Pipe Works was the only photo available. It is unfortunate that actual photos of this area don't exist.

Photo of Black-Horse Works one-half mile south of New Cumberland
Photo courtesy of Mack Manufacturing

These are the only photos of these plants we were able to locate. With the exception of the Black-Horse Works, it appears that the Mack Manufacturing Company was the only company that took actual photographs of their plants.

WEST VIRGINIA FIRE CLAY COMPANY, NEW CUMBERLAND

WV Fire Clay replaced the N.W. Ballantyne Clay Grinding Company
Photo courtesy of Brick and Clay Record, page 167

The above sketch of the N. W. Ballantyne Clay Company is the only diagram/sketch that could be found of for this facility. Several actual pictures were located, but they were of such poor quality we couldn't include them in this book. We did, however, find photos of the Ballantyne brothers.

NATHANIEL W. BALLANTYNE,
Secretary.

C. A. BALLANTYNE,
Manager.

Photos of N.W. and C.A. Ballantyne
Photo courtesy of Ohio Valley Manufacturer

The brothers Nathaniel W., for whom the plant was named, and Charles A. were the registered owners. Nathaniel was secretary and Charles plant manager. According to published records, this clay processing plant was extremely profitable. Started in 1898 as a clay crushing plant, it continued operations until closing in 1963. It was located at the bottom of Ballantyne Road just outside of New Cumberland.

By 1923, all the brickyards south of New Cumberland had stopped operating, and by 1942 all the buildings from these brickyards were completely torn down with the exception of the West Virginia Fire Clay Company.

Chapter Six
Brickmaking North of New Cumberland

Likewise, at the northern part of New Cumberland, a couple of brickyards, between 1904 and 1909, had stopped producing brick or sewer pipe. Those included Clifton, Eagle, and Globe. Rockyside and Etna continued operating until sometime in late 1930. During this time period, all these plants were under ownership of Crescent Brick Company. The Etna yard was closed around 1950, leaving the Crescent and Union plants operating. Crescent closed and all buildings were removed in 1965. The Union plant was the last to close in early 1980 after the Crescent clay mine on Hardins Run Road was closed in late 1979.

Photo taken from the Ohio side looking at the Union Brickyard in 1976
Photo courtesy of George Hines

Brickyards as they were located north of New Cumberland started with the Mack Manufacturing Office at what is now the intersection of Routes 2 and 8. In order progressing north: Clifton Works, Crescent Brick, Etna, Cunningham & Taylor, Eagle, Union, Rockyside, and finally Globe brickyards. These plants were situated in an area that covered roughly two and one-half miles along the Ohio River, ending at the bottom of Globe Hill.

167

Photo of Mack Office north of New Cumberland
Photo courtesy of Mack Manufacturing

Photo of Clifton Lower sewer pipe yard just south of Mack Office
Photo courtesy of Mack Manufacturing

This photo taken sometime in early 1900 shows the old Mack Office and the Clifton Works in the background. A new Mack Office would eventually be built. To the right of the photo is the tipple for the Crescent mine. This would be the first Crescent mine located near where the intersection of Routes 2 and 8 is currently located.

168

Photo of the Crescent plant and old Route 66
Photo courtesy of Mack Manufacturing

Photo of the backside of the Clifton Works facing south
Photo courtesy of Mack Manufacturing

Photo of the Clifton Works facing north from the river
Photo courtesy of Mack Manufacturing

Photo of the Crescent plant – sewer pipe from Clifton Upper Works – Clay tipples from the Etna and Crescent mines – The area directly under the clay tipples and partially seen in the distance is old Route 66
Photo courtesy of Mack Manufacturing

Photo is of the backside of the Crescent plant looking south from the river –
Crescent clay tipple is shown to the upper left
Photo courtesy of Mack Manufacturing

Photo of the Etna plant looking north – just north of the Crescent plant
The large building to the left is the brick drying building
Photo courtesy of The Brick – Volume 29, page 507

*Photo of a closer look of the clay pile at the bottom of the Etna clay tipples –
Route 66 runs under the tipples - arrow shows it in upper left*
Photo courtesy of The Brick – Volume 29, page 507

Photo of Etna plant looking north showing more kilns
Photo courtesy of Mack Manufacturing

Photo of the Eagle sewer pipe plant just north of the Etna plant
Photo courtesy of Mack Manufacturing

Photo of the Eagle plant looking north to see the Union Brickyard – observe
how close the Ohio River is to the plants
Photo courtesy of Mack Manufacturing

Photo of the Union Brickyard – observe large house on top of hill
Arrow points to brick drying building
Photo courtesy of Mack Manufacturing

Photo of the Union Brickyard
Photo courtesy of Mack Manufacturing

174

Photo - one of two steam shovels purchased by Mack in 1912
Photo courtesy of Hancock County Courier

Photo of Union Clay Crusher building – date unknown
Large object on top of the building is part of the clay tipple
Photo courtesy of Ed Reese

Photo of Union Clay Crusher building – date unknown
Photo courtesy of Ed Reese

Photo of Union Clay Crusher building today (2017)
Photo courtesy of T. W. Zielinsky

Photo of Union Clay Crusher building side view
Photos courtesy of T. W. Zielinsky

Photo of the Union Clay Crusher building backside view
Photo courtesy of T. W. Zielinsky

177

Photo of Rockyside Brickyard – clay crushing/mechanical building in the foreground while actual brickmaking yard is in the background
Photo courtesy of Mack Manufacturing

At the top right side of the photo you can see a railroad track coming from the Union Brickyard. The Rockyside plant is where this railroad track ends.

Photo of Rockyside Brickyard north of the clay crushing building
Photo courtesy of Mack Manufacturing

Photo of first Globe Brickyard north of New Cumberland at the bottom of
Globe Hill next to the Ohio River
Photo courtesy of The Brick – Volume 29, page 389

Photo of first Globe Brickyard looking from the hillside facing south toward
New Cumberland – Photo courtesy of Mack Manufacturing

There is really nothing left of what was once the brickmaking capital of West Virginia. These brickyards were either destroyed by fire or collapsed under their own weight; they are gone, never coming back to life. The next generation

179

and the generation after that will probably never know where these giant brick beehives once stood or that they even existed. The only remains left behind is the clay crusher building of the Union brickyard. Some kiln bases and a few bricks from a couple of chimneys are all that is left standing. It is surprising that what is still standing will probably remain for years unless someone comes along to develop the land. What is currently standing will become buried like the remains of Rockyside.

The Horse Trail

So many items of interest were uncovered while I was doing this research, and I realized how much history has gone away. When I sat down with my cousin Gertrude Ludovici, she mentioned something about a horse trail, and how this horse trail led behind and up past the brickyards and the back of the Zumer home. It started next to the brickyard floor and proceeded upward at an angle. It was how coal and supplies were moved from the bottom to the top of the hill.

What was even more surprising was her comment that you can actually still see this horse trail from the Ohio side of the river. So, my wife and I went on a road trip. Once we could see the Union brickyard, we were amazed that we could actually see the contour of the hillside leading up from the brickyard floor to just past where we located the Zumer foundation. There was a part of the hillside that was missing just before where the clay crusher building stood. After over a hundred years, the majority of the trail is still there. Just past the Zumer foundation, another part of the incline was missing because the hillside had been altered to close the Union clay mine, so that part of the trail is gone. I'm not sure how much farther the trail went past the Union clay crusher building. I guess no one will ever know. However, railroad tracks that ran alongside the horse trail extended all the way to the Rockyside plant.

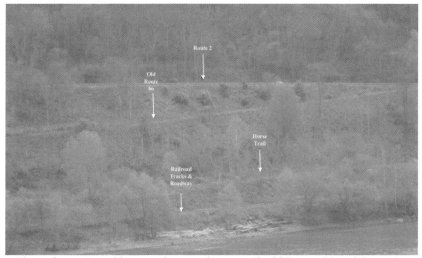

Photo shows 4 road layers – bottom, horse trail, old Route 66 and Route 2
Photo taken April 2016 courtesy of T. W. Zielinsky

This photo captures, from the Ohio side, four different layers showing the brickyard roadway, the horse trail, old Route 66, and finally Route 2 on the top.

The next photo shows the incline from the brickyard floor, standing on the roadway, just about where the Eagle plant was located. The horse trail starts about where the Crescent plant ended and the Etna plant started, which is located south toward New Cumberland.

Photo taken on the brickyard roadway showing the incline – photo was taken about where the Eagle plant would have been located

This next photo is about where the horse trail begins, roughly at north end of the Crescent Brickyard. In the foreground, you can see indentions where the railroad tracks were installed. These railroad tracks extend all the way to the Rockyside Brickyard, over a mile away. The pile on the left is burnt and used brick.

Photo of the start of where the horse trail begins – facing north
Photo courtesy of T. W. Zielinsky

Photo on top of the horse trail facing south – brick pile now on the right
Photo courtesy of T. W. Zielinsky

182

This part of the horse trail is fairly level and rises only several feet from the actual roadway. From this point forward, the incline begins to increase in elevation and then levels off and becomes flat for a couple of hundred yards.

Photo showing the very top of the horse trail – railroad tracks are still in place and copper colored water to the left hillside indicates the present of clay mine activity – photo looking south – Photo courtesy of T. W. Zielinsky

Photo on top of the horse trail from the exact spot from the previous photo now looking north – the angle of steepness continues to rise
Photo courtesy of T. W. Zielinsky

The spot where these last two pictures were taken would be about midway into the brickyard property near what was the Eagle plant. The next photo will move you forward into the Union plant, and the only remaining tipple that rests on top of the horse trail. I placed a marker on the above photo as to the location of the tipple, which is barely visible in the photo.

Just past this tipple is where the horse trail breaks away from the hillside. This was intentionally done to close the Union Clay mine and remove the incline and associated railroad tracks. When this action happened is unknown, but this picture taken in the late 1950's shows the hillside already altered and cleared away.

Photo of Union Brickyard sometime in late 1950 – hillside has already been cleared, mines have been sealed and closed, railroad track and incline were removed - Photo courtesy of George Hines

In the early 1960's, clay was being transferred from the Crescent Mine on Hardins Run Road and brought to the brickyard by trucks. You can see the trucks in the front of the tipple in the photo. The white substance on the bank of the Ohio River is broken bricks that were discarded.

184

Photo of last remaining clay/coal tipple near the Union plant which rests on top of the horse trail – Photo courtesy of T. W. Zielinsky

The Union plant produced brick until 1980 by using clay from the Crescent Clay Mine on Hardins Run Road. When this clay mine closed in 1979, the Union plant closed shortly thereafter. The photo below shows the horse trail cut away. It picks back up about half way past the storage building then proceeds past the Zumer foundation.

Photo of horse trail cut away from the hillside
Photo courtesy of T. W. Zielinsky

185

Photo of Horse Trail continuing up the side of the hill
Photo courtesy of T. W. Zielinsky

Photo of the Horse Trail continuing up behind the Zumer foundation
Photo Courtesy of T. W. Zielinsky

The horse trail finally ends just past this spot in the photo on the hillside. The hillside levels off up to the clay crusher building. The hillside behind the clay crusher building has also been plowed under.

Photo of the Horse Trail running behind the Zumer foundation

This is the only physical remains of the Mack Manufacturing Company and Crescent Brick Company brickyards.

Photo of the remains of the Crescent brickyard kilns/chimneys
Photos courtesy of T. W. Zielinsky

187

Chapter Seven
The first Catholic Church and School

The first Catholic Church was built on Rockyside in 1904 with permission from the Bishop of Wheeling, WV, and the Mack Manufacturing Company. The Mack Company allowed the church to be built because of the number of Catholic immigrants and the fact that no Catholic church was available in this area.

The dimensions of the church, based on extrapolation, would be 20 feet wide by 40 feet long. This is based on four-foot wide steps leading up to the front door. The church was made entirely from wood with a slate roof and a brick and sewer pipe foundation.

Photo of the first Catholic Church on Rockyside in 1904
Photo courtesy of Dave and Bonnie Burskey

The following transcript is taken from the actual newspaper article that started the effort to build the church. The article was run in a Catholic newspaper called *The Catholic Calendar*. This newspaper was eventually replaced by *The Catholic Spirit*, which is published today keeping Catholics informed about church and dioceses activities.

The article, dated September 1904, read as follows:

A New Mission
New Cumberland to Have a Resident Priest

Some weeks ago, Rt. Rev. Bishop Donahue, accompanied by Rev. E. Musial, pastor of St. Stanislaus's Parish, Wheeling, made a visit of inspection to the Northern Panhandle to see what could be done for the spiritual needs of the many Poles and Slavs said to be employed in that neighborhood. About two miles outside of New Cumberland, almost on the summit of a lofty ridge overlooking the Ohio up and down stream, they found a colony of Poles, employees of a pottery company living under singular if not unique conditions in that secluded neighborhood. There were some two hundred men, all unmarried. There is one woman only in the immediate neighborhood. All the men take their meals together in one great building and sleep in another equally large which is called the "Barracks." The company pays each one-dollar and a half a day and deducts a third of that sum for board and lodging so that the workers' savings may be almost twice their expenses. The officials of the company showed great courtesy to the visitors and at great trouble went over the ground selecting a site for a neat little church.

As a result, Rt. Rev. Bishop Donahue has appointed Rev. Julius Javorek pastor of the new mission. This young priest has been ordained but a few months and has been assisting Rev. E. Musial. He seems particularly encouraged with the prospects of the new mission and hopes to be in position to begin the erection of a new church with the next few weeks. The company has kindly consented to give him all the land he desires and to help in other ways. The site is ideal. Rev. Julius Javorek is at present boarding with Mrs. Kelly, a venerable lady, who has in the past extended gracious hospitality to the visiting clergy. Father Javorek does not understand a single word of English and Mrs. Kelly is equally innocent of Polish. This state of affairs naturally leads to some international complications for the time being, but is being gradually relieved. – End of article

A search to find more information about Mrs. Kelly came up empty. I was not able to find one person who knew anything about this Mrs. Kelly or where she lived. Apparently, she lived somewhere close to the Rockyside hillside, possibly in the very northern part of New Cumberland.

Father Julius Javorek served as pastor from 1904 until 1910. Nothing was found as to why Father Javorek left or where he relocated. For the next ten years, Immaculate Conception Church served as a mission church and was pastored by visiting priests.

In 1920, the Most Reverend Patrick Donahue, Bishop of Wheeling, WV, appointed the Reverend Father Francis Olszewski pastor of this church. He would hold services on Rockyside for the next 14 years. Records do not indicate where Father Olszewski's residence was located during this time.

Photo of Father Francis Olszewski
Photo courtesy of John Kuzio

In 1921, Father Olszewski saw a need for a Catholic School in New Cumberland and found a 100-year-old structure on North Water Street, or North River Avenue. Today it's known as North River Street. It was formerly used as a hotel/boarding house that was deeded initially to Mr. William Matthewson on April 1, 1850. The property changed hands

191

over the years until finally it was acquired by Father Olszewski on August 1, 1921, Deed Book 34/189.

Photo of the back of the Catholic School around 1904
Photo courtesy of Greg Blake

I'm not sure when the above photo was actually taken, but the foreground is the new Lock No.9 Dam, which was under construction in 1904. The foreground shows newly poured concrete, so it is assumed to be around 1904 when the hotel underwent renovations, as the entire back of the building is under construction. I've pointed out the placement of the water well. Eventually, dirt with a brick floor (yard) will be put in place, a fenced-in area known to us as our playground, and at the back of the yard, facing the river, would be two outside bathrooms, one for the boys and the other for the girls.

This photo, shows an extremely large amount of dirt/fill was needed to be put in place to make the yard flat. The yard would extend about 20 yards past the well to reach the end of the yard and fence.

County Assessor records indicate that from 1888 to 1917 Dora M. Stewart, Deed G/456, owned the property. John A. Richardson purchased the property in 1917, Deed 30/296, and
192

held the property until May 1920 when it was purchased by J. W. Robb & Harry Sprague, Deed 33/32. They soon sold it to Father Olszewski on August 1, 1920, to be renovated and turned into a school.

After it was renovated, the building contained two classrooms on the first floor. The first-grade room was on the right side, in the back of the building facing toward the river. The larger classroom was also on the right side, but at the front of the building. Two additional rooms were on the left, and these were the kitchen and the sitting room. Upstairs to the left was a small chapel, and on the right side of the building were several bedrooms. Water was brought in from the well and placed in a 5-gallon container with a push faucet. The building did have electricity and several potbelly coal stoves to keep us warm, but in general the building was cold.

The school was run by nuns from the Sisters Auxiliaries of the Apostolate, an order that Father Olszewski was instrumental in organizing. Their home was in Monongah, WV. A total of six nuns lived in the school from 1921 until 1955, when the school finally closed. In addition to Sisters Arsenia and Dolores, there were Sisters Ursula, Clara, Joseph, and Veronica.

   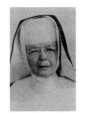

Sister Mary Arsenia (1921-1955)*   Sister Mary Dolores (1933-1955)*   Sister Mary Ursula (1921-1922)*   Sister Mary Clara (1922-1930)*

Sister Mary Joseph (1924-1933)*   Sister Mary Veronica (1924-1925)*

(*) Indicates years teaching at Immaculate Conception School
Photos courtesy of John Kuzio

193

All of these nuns are now deceased. In first grade, everyone had Sister Arsenia as a teacher. All I can say is that she was strict! Very, very strict! I'll leave it at that.

Second through eighth grades were in the larger classroom with each row of desks being a grade. Sister Dolores was the teacher for all remaining grades, two through eight. What was nice was the ability to hear what she was teaching to the other grades. Before you knew it, you were learning what the higher grades were learning. It's amazing that this principle isn't used in our school systems today.

Sister Arsenia was born in 1879 and died 1966, and Sister Dolores was born in 1912 and died 1989.

Photo back of school – Sister Mary Dolores on the left and Sister Mary Arsenia on the right – Photo courtesy of Mike Peterson

This photo is of Sister Dolores and Sister Arsenia standing on a small porch at the back of the school. Please take note of the brick courtyard alongside of where they are standing. This brick courtyard extended all the way to the back of the property.

My uncle Fred Mack purchased the school building in July of 1959. He wanted to make it into an apartment building, but the building was eventually torn down. It had deteriorated to the point that no number of repairs would make the building into what he wanted. So, he decided to just tear it down.

Photo of the front of the one-room Catholic schoolhouse on North River Avenue just prior to being torn down – Photo courtesy of Mike Peterson

The above photo shows the front of the Catholic school building that Father Olszewski started. Railroad tracks in the foreground were located just outside the front door.

In 1934, Father Olszewski requested a new church be built in New Cumberland because most of the families were moving off Rockyside into town. He received permission once again from the Bishop, and the process started by dismantling the church on Rockyside and bringing the materials into town. The church was built on the corner of North Chester and Jackson Streets on Nazarene Church property.

John Kuzio described how everything from the Rockyside church was dismantled, piece-by-piece, brick-by-brick, and taken into New Cumberland to be later used for the

195

new church. Men such as Lucas Simon, John Kuzio, Sr., Joe Stolarczyk, and John Zielinski, along with other parishioners helped carry the material for the new church to the building site.

The Rockyside church took less than four months to complete. The new church, started in 1934, took nearly four years to complete. During this period, the parishioners attended church in the upstairs chapel in the school. The new church was dedicated on Christmas Day 1938. The original wooden rectory, built in 1934, was completely destroyed by the 1936 flood and would be rebuilt soon after, but with bricks and physically attached to the new church.

A picture was featured in a local newspaper called *The Independent*, on March 19, 1936, showing the rectory flipped upside down by floodwaters. The picture was of such poor quality I chose not to include it. The caption under the picture read: *"This is a view of Rev. Fr. Olszewski residence, upset. Located in upper town, south of Peoples Store building. The Polish Priest lost another house and it landed in the Dr. Beaumont lot in lower town."*

Photo of second Catholic Church – church is on right, rectory on left

Photo of second church remodeled in 1955 that included a church addition

Photo shows church extension completed in 1955
All church photos courtesy of John Kuzio

Eventually, a new (third Catholic Church) would be built on Ridge Avenue. It was started in 1966 and was finished and dedicated on May 4, 1969.

Chapter Eight
Other Manufacturing in
New Cumberland

This photo of the Duraloy Company was found by George Hines and is a little unusual. In this undated photo, the building can be seen from the site of the New Cumberland Dam Locks. It must have been taken shortly after being built in 1916. Most of upper town, along North Chestnut Street, hasn't been built yet. This photo was taken before the Duraloy name was painted on the roof.

Photo of Duraloy Company date unknown – *Photo courtesy of George Hines*

No other pictures could be found that represented the other manufacturing that occurred in New Cumberland.

This section does contain a photo of Mr. Thomas R. Heyward, Jr., founder of the Cutler Steel/Duraloy Company, along with an overview of the history of this company as it relates specifically to New Cumberland. Mr. Vince Schiavoni, current President of Duraloy, provided the historical information. The actual article is exceptionally long, and the majority of information doesn't pertain to New Cumberland, so only the information about New Cumberland has been provided. To consider that this manufacturing process started in New Cumberland and still continues today after almost 80 years is amazing.

Cutler Steel Company₁ - 1921

The Cutler Steel Company began in 1921 in Pittsburgh as a companion to a steel foundry located in New Cumberland that was founded by Thomas R. Heyward, Jr. The New Cumberland foundry was built to make heat-treated steel castings. Heyward received a license in that same year to produce an iron alloy that was made of 30 per cent chrome and named his product DURALOY. The name was a combination of the two words durable and alloy. This new alloy was designed to resist high temperatures, corrosion, and abrasion. The name of the new company Cutler was chosen because the first proposed product was hoped to be specially heat-treated steel for the cutlery trade.

When the company began, Heyward was the sole owner, and he arranged funding for the business by selling shares to some personal friends. His product was slow in production, and progress was not up to his initial expectations. However, Heyward was still optimistic about his prospects. Around the same time, another company in Pittsburgh developed a similar product and gave Heyward the license to produce it at the New Cumberland foundry.

Heyward wanted to start production immediately before any other companies could produce a similar product. But development and sales of the product were so slow that debts began to mount, and the company was forced to stop production. Business conditions were bad all over the country, and small businesses such as this one didn't stand much of a chance. With no money left, Heyward was forced to close the plant in New Cumberland for an indefinite period.

In 1925, the company was still in business but still facing hard economic times as well as sales resistance and lack of funds. DURALOY had made some progress in developing a demand for its product, and the company hired a new manager to oversee the foundry in New Cumberland. In September 1925, the plant was back in operation. Work continued at the plant for several months with moderate but encouraging results. That is when management decided to buy the plant

200

and its assets from the creditors and acquire sole rights to the trade name DURALOY. Heyward became the sole owner once again and operated the plant until 1937 when it was destroyed by fire. Still not one to give up, Heyward bought an abandoned plant in Scottdale, PA, and moved his foundry to this new location.

This plant is still in operation but has change ownership several times. White Consolidated Industries Inc. of Cleveland purchased the assets in 1974 who then sold it to Blawknox Corporation in 1985. The current owners, Cleveland-based Park Corporation, purchased Duraloy in 1994. The company does business all over the world and still makes heat-resistant alloys similar to the ones that were originally made at its first foundry in New Cumberland, West Virginia.

The above information was supplied to me from a book that was written by Thomas Rhett Heyward, Jr., titled *History of the Duraloy Company*[1] covering a period from 1921 to 1953. Current President of Duraloy and the person who supplied the book information is Vince Schiavoni. The book has some 136 pages with about 8 photographs, one of them the New Cumberland plant that I've included in this book. Since Vince indicated to me that he couldn't let the book out of his sight, he was gracious enough to copy the first 20 pages that dealt specifically with the New Cumberland facility and early company problems.

What I also found interesting is that Duraloy finds success after nearly 80 years in business and is still going strong. A narrative was posted on the *TribLive* home page dated April 27, 2012, that praised the company's 75th year in business. It stated, in part;

"The first batch of superhard iron-chrome alloy was melted in a foundry now operated by Duraloy Technologies Inc., in Scottdale, PA, 75 years ago this month.

The company, which employs 90 workers, is one of only a few that produces composites of chrome, nickel, and iron that can withstand high temperatures needed for furnaces used in the oil, chemical, and steel industries

Duraloy, owned by Cleveland-based Park Corp., has expanded under that ownership, shipping products worth $53 million last year. Workers can produce more than 200 recipes of blended metals, but usually stick to about 75 to make semi-finished or completely finished products for customers.

The company does business worldwide with customers in the United States, Mexico, Canada, Netherlands, Korea, India and Middle East countries.

With the company now at its most successful point, its goals are to continue expansion and upgrades to the Duraloy plant."

Photo of Thomas Rhett Heyward, Jr. (1881 – 1954)
Founder of the Cutler Steel/Duraloy Company

Mr. Thomas R. Heyward, Jr., was 73 when he passed away in 1954. He was married to Marguerite Busch Heyward. They had two sons, Thomas Rhett Heyward III who passed away at the age of 88 on December 1, 2003, and Robert Benjamin Heyward who passed away also at the age of 88 on October 25, 2006.

Both sons worked for the company. Thomas was elevated to President and Chairman of the Board, while brother Robert was Vice President of Engineering and Technical Director.

Chapter Nine
The Zumer and Zielinsky Families

All photos are included in the Book Section.

Chapter Ten
A Tribute to the Brick "King"

All photos are included in the Book Section.

Epilogue

Writing a book is never easy and requires a lot of fortitude and determination. I found that out on my first book adventure.

My first book was hard, but this book was even harder. I had a ton of information for my first book, so it made the challenge somewhat easier. Most of the material I used in the first book was in journals that I kept or in annual reports published by the company.

This book about Rockyside was much more difficult because I really didn't have any information when I started. Some information was available either on-line or in books at the library regarding brickyards, clay mining, or making brick, but it was in small little chunks. There were very few pictures and not many people around who actually lived on top of that barren hillside. It has been like putting together a jigsaw puzzle but without having a picture to guide you along.

But, sitting down, I made a list of what I thought I was going to need. First thing on my list were names and phone numbers of people I needed to contact. Next I came up with a short list of questions I needed to ask. The first person on the list was John Kuzio. And so it began.

John and I met for our first of many two-hour sessions. Each question I asked led to another question and then another question, and it went on and on. It seemed I was generating more questions than I was getting answers. Then, after my first meeting with my cousin Gertrude Ludovici, I realized I needed to begin laying all the information out and try to form a picture of what I was hoping to accomplish. That's how it continued, day after day.

Each person I talked with would tell me about someone else I should try contacting. Starting with just that one person led me to three-dozen or more contacts. Each day would reveal something different. Each day I would put something new on my computer diagram, or maybe I would take something off. This process continued week after week for nearly two years. Finally, a picture began to take shape.

What I learned through yet another book writing experience is patience and the belief that the creator of the universe is helping to guide me. That's how this experience resonates with me. There were dozens of people, some offering only a tiny bit of information, but that small bit would lead to something spectacular.

Just to provide a small insight into what I'm talking about, here are a few examples I feel are noteworthy. I was given mine payroll journals with names and the exact year my grandfathers started working on Rockyside. Then I crossed paths with the owner of the brickyard property who just happened to have original mine maps. Having a picture of a home sitting on top of a hill, with a faint image of a steeple in the background, would lead to the discovery of where the first Catholic Church was built. I had all the right people come to my aid at just the right moment in time to provide me with yet another piece of critical information, like the only picture to that first church. I believe everything was timed exactly for me in digestible pieces. Each piece had a purpose and was put in place before the next piece became available.

Everything I've done with the project has been timed to an exact moment in time. It's like I was somehow preordained to write this book. Initially I was just going to write a book about growing up in New Cumberland, and now look what I've done. I have been in the right place, at the right time, to put all of this together with all the right people. I truly know what being blessed feels like.

The blessings I received from being with all the special people who came to help has been truly amazing. Even to have a very finicky grammarian come, who just appeared to fix my not so good English, is a blessing.

Writing this book has made me realize the great hardships and struggles these families must have endured as they lived without any of our modern conveniences. People back then appeared to care for and help one another more than people are willing to do today. Writing the book made me aware of my own down to earth core principles that I learned at a young age, of working hard and being kind and caring. These principles seemed to have skipped the next several generations completely. I was expected to do well in everything I set out to accomplish, not so much for me but to make my parents just a little proud. I know that the principles they learned would also carry on to me and be further passed down to my children. But somewhere in time those principles have stopped. The world just isn't like it used to be.

I hope everything I learned has helped me to write this book, like believe in myself completely and the task I'm trying to accomplish. I learned to believe in the people around me and know they have been put there for a reason. Those people who responded to me, in any way, were meant to be part of this experience. Those people who didn't respond missed an opportunity.

So, be open and honest with yourself on what you are trying to achieve. Focus your basic belief system on completing the task at hand, take deep breaths along the way, and let the creator help lead you. This is why I stated at the beginning of the book, that New Cumberland is such a great town, a great place to live, and all because of the people. Thank you New Cumberland for this amazing experience.

Glossary of Terms

Blake Crusher[13] – On June 15, 1858, Eli Whitney Blake of New Haven, Connecticut, was granted US patent No. 20,542 for a "machine for crushing stone." Eli is the nephew of cotton-gin inventor Eli Whitney. This machine allows large stones to be crushed into smaller pieces, even down to a dust.

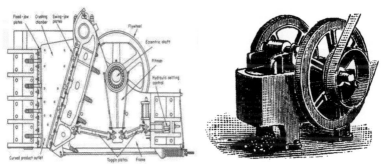

Blake Crusher

Bricks – Bricks produced in the early years were done each to their own, meaning each brickyard stamped their own name into their respective product. The Mack Manufacturing Company was not an exception to this rule. Their special paving brick was not only used for streets but also for building large structures such as homes.

They were unique in design that one side was beveled so that when it was laid down on a street, it would be easier on the horses' and mules' legs and hooves. The top of the brick had two ridges about 3/8 inches in height to allow for an interlocking to take place. Finally, there was a hollow groove on the backside and the two ends that was also used for interlocking the bricks when the bricks were laid down.

Photos of Mack Bricks with logo and ridges on top and backside showing grooves on the bottom and sides of the brick

Photo of Porter's Eagle Works Brick
Brick courtesy of Jim Caldwell

The Porter's Eagle Works Brick was a truly rare find made by my friend Jim Caldwell. Jim was working a job in Wellsburg and came across this brick. He knew that I was putting this book together and did receive permission from the homeowner before walking away with the brick. The reason the brick is rare is the Eagle plant only operated as a brickyard for a short period before being converted into making just sewer pipe.

Photo of a Rockyside Brick with RS stamped into the brick
Brick courtesy of George Hines

Brickmaking Machinery[16] – Brick making machinery was used in the production of all brick. These machines varied in style and complexity. Some very crude machines were initially used until manufacturers understood that making brick would be around for the foreseeable future. Then more elaborate machines were invented that could produce hundreds of bricks per hour.

The process was to grind the clay and process it with water. The wet clay was then placed into an extrusion machine that would form the bricks. Once the bricks were formed, they were set to dry and then fired in the dome kilns in order to cure the clay. The resulting product was firebrick.

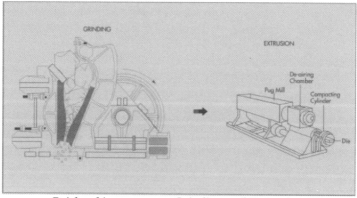

Brickmaking process – Grinding and Extrusion
These two processes turn clay into actual bricks

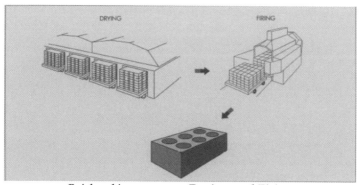

Brickmaking process – Drying, and Firing
These two processes allow the brick first to dry then they are heated for the curing to be complete

Clay Working[1] – Clay working was the most important part of brickmaking, and it consisted of either Kittanning or Clarion clays. The type of clay used determined the type of brick or sewer pipe being made.

The clay was dug from the hillsides underground through tunnel openings starting at the bottom of the hillside slightly up from the Ohio River. Other clay seams were found higher up in the hillsides and extended from the bottom of Globe Hill, along the river's bend, into New Cumberland and finally out onto Hardins Run Road.

Clay was dug and moved out of the mines by gravity, but sometime mules or horses were used to pull the cars to the tipples where the clay was dumped next to the brickyard and left to dry. Once the clay was screened to remove rocks, the clay and some shale were ground into powder by a crusher or "clapper" as it was called.

Water was added to the clay, clay powder, and sand, which was then soaked, stirred, and kneaded with large augers or wooden paddles until it became like a dough. This process was called tempering or pugging, and was the hardest work of all. In the mid-1800's, horse driven pug mills were invented. The clay was removed from the pug mill by a "temperer" who delivered it to the moulding area for forming.

Corliss Engine[2] – A Corliss engine was a steam engine, fitted with rotary valves and with variable valve timing. It was patented in 1849 and invented by and named after the American engineer George Henry Corliss of Providence, Rhode Island.

Engines fitted with Corliss valve gear offered the best thermal efficiency of any type of stationary steam engine until the refinement of the uniflow steam engine and steam turbine in the 20th century. Corliss engines were generally about 30 percent more fuel efficient than conventional steam engines with fixed cutoff. This increased efficiency made steam power more economical than waterpower, allowing industrial development away from millponds.

Corliss engines were typically used as stationary engines to provide mechanical power to line shafting power in factories and mills and to drive dynamos to generate electricity. Many were quite large, standing many meters tall and developing several hundred horsepower, albeit at low speed, and turning massive flywheels weighing several tons at about 100 revolutions per minute. Some of these engines had unusual roles as mechanical legacy systems and because of their relatively high efficiency and low maintenance requirements.

Note: Because of the proximity of the brickyards to the Ohio River, it made it convenient to use Corliss engines with an abundance of available river water – Mack Manufacturing had a total of 26 steam boilers in operation to supply the Corliss engines they utilized

Corliss Engine 1904

Crib[10] - The crib is the roof support of propped up timbers or railroad ties, laid in alternate cross-layers, log-cabin style. It may or may not be filled with debris (shale). The debris was to add security to the timbers.

Cyrus Chambers[3] – Cyrus Chamber of Philadelphia invented another type brickmaking machine in 1863. It used stiff mud (clay) which was forced out in long ribbons on a conveyor belt, transferred to molds, and cut by a revolving cutter. As time progressed, up to 25 bricks could be cut at a time. The bricks were then stamped with the appropriate name or design.

Downdraft Kilns[19]– These kilns, similar to the Eu Daly Kilns, were a rounded dome or beehive shape, formed entirely out of brick. On the outside of the kiln, in order to keep the brick from expanding, large steel bands were placed around the bricks to keep the beehive intact. A large metal door with locking steel plates was installed which allowed one-way in and one-way out. Once the bricks were placed inside, the door was closed and locked before heat was applied to the furnace.

Photo of downdraft kiln – Crescent Works
Photo courtesy of Mack Manufacturing

Photo of downdraft kiln – Crescent Works – Taken 1920
Notice heavy steel bands and turnbuckle over doorway
Left to Right: Matt McKenna, Roy Baker, Tom Knox, Dan Fickes,
Harry Sprague, Cleve Friman, Dick Staley, George Robb, and Unknown
Photo courtesy of Mack Manufacturing

214

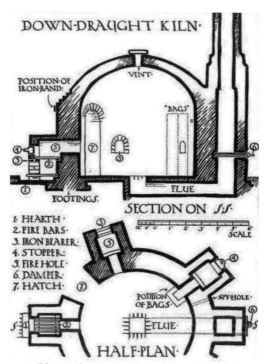

Photo of cross-section of downdraft kiln
Photo courtesy of The Brick and Clay Record, Volume 12, page 345

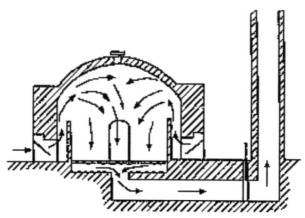

Photo of airflow in a downdraft kiln
Photo courtesy of https://en.wikipedia.org/wiki/downdraft kiln

Dry Pans[17] – Dry pans were used in clay processing as a means of refining the clay prior to mixing. These pans caught the clay as a series of screens sifted the clay into finer and finer consistency.

Drying Beds[18] – These drying beds were built of brick with hot-air tunnels underneath. They were typically built adjacent to the clay processing buildings and were nearly 100 feet long and 45 feet wide. Hot-air was forced into approximately 10 tunnels under the floor, with each tunnel having its own furnace. Average drying time was between 18 and 24 hours prior to the firing process.

Eu Daly Kilns[4] – Eu Daly Kilns were invented by William A. Eudaly from Cincinnati, Ohio, and were patented November 7, 1893. These kilns were in use at various brickyards both north and south of New Cumberland in the early days of brickmaking. They improved the burning of all kinds of clay and clay wares. These downdraft kilns improved and created a more equal distribution of heat, giving more uniformity in burning, a more perfect combustion, and producing greater economy of fuel and labor.

Each furnace had a double crown with an air chamber between the upper and lower crowns. The air chambers were adapted to convey the external air to the products of combustion in the combustion chamber situated within the kiln proper by means of air fines entirely exterior to the furnace or furnace throat.

The kiln had double bag walls situated within the kiln, and air-chambers between these two walls each connected with the external air by means of air fines situated at the bottom of the chamber. It also had a system of hot air flues and chambers located in positions that allowed the external air to pass through. The Eu Daly kilns improved how a kiln was built and included rounded bag walls for improved heat transfer efficiency.

Next is the actual diagram of the patent received on November 7, 1893 by William A. Eudaly.

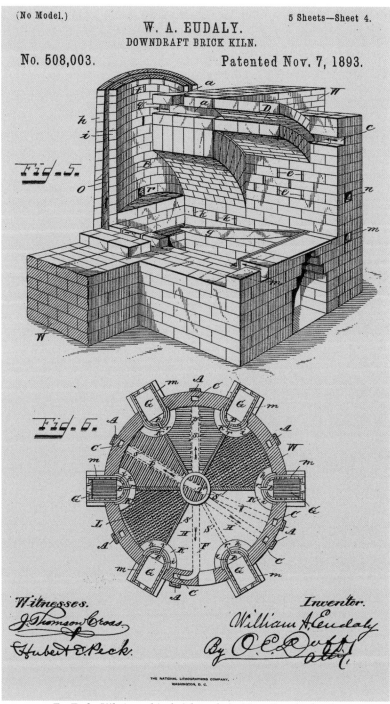

(No Model.)

W. A. EUDALY.
DOWNDRAFT BRICK KILN.

5 Sheets—Sheet 4.

No. 508,003.

Patented Nov. 7, 1893.

Fig-5.

Fig. 6.

Witnesses.

J. Thomson Cross

Hubert E. Peck.

Inventor.

William A. Eudaly

By O. C. Duffy
Atty.

Eu Daly Kiln⁴ used in brickyards in New Cumberland

217

Jumper[10] – A Jumper was an iron chisel with a steel point and was 18 to 24 inches long. It was used to make holes in the wall of a mine where dynamite was inserted. The blast caused by the dynamite caused the clay to be broken into large pieces for loading into clay cars.

Kittanning Clay[5] – Kittanning clay and Clarion clay are extremely abundant throughout the Hancock County area, especially in and near where the brickyards were built. In just about all the books and other material printed about the brickyards referenced these Kittanning and Clarion clays.

Around 1830, Kittanning fire clays, also known as flint clays, were first mined at the mouth of Holberts Run. So what is Kittanning fire clay? Kittanning and Clarion are names associated with clay that comes from towns of the same name in eastern part of Pennsylvania just east of Pittsburgh. They are considered first and foremost coal seams and extend from the Kittanning and Clarion areas into the panhandle of West Virginia and eastern parts of Ohio in areas known as quadrangles.

This clay was formed some 325 to 290 million years ago in an era when much of our area was a low-lying area repeatedly inundated by ocean waters. Eroded soil and minerals from the highland rocks washed down and were deposited in the shallow water bottoms. Then, at intervals many hundreds of thousands of years later, the waters receded and lush vegetation covered the landscape. Gradually the climatic conditions reversed, and the waters returned, killing the vegetation. As time progressed, the eroded sediment covered the decayed vegetation. Eventually the decayed vegetation would turn into coal, and the eroded sediments would form a layer of various types of clay, or it would form some rock-type formation.

Due to the various amounts and types of soils and minerals that were eroded and deposited at each interval, all of the clay layers have some distinguishing characteristics. One of these clays known as Lower Kittanning was found to be particularly useful in making stoneware. Kittanning is high-grade, buff or yellowish colored, plastic clay with few impurities. The white clays also known as Lower Kittanning contain a relative small amount of iron oxide.

218

There are actually three types of Kittanning coal and associated clays: the Lower Kittanning, Middle Kittanning, and Upper Kittanning coal and respective clay seams. Coal sits on top of an underlining clay seam. Lower Kittanning coal and clay seams are very abundant through Ohio and Pennsylvania, but in West Virginia the coal seams are absent entirely down to a 3-8 foot height as a workable bed. But in their place are large amounts of fire clay. In Hancock County, the Lower Kittanning clay under the coal will range from 7 to 20 feet thick and average about 16 feet. The coal seam on top of the clay averages about 3-8 feet thick, and the sandstone on top of the coal averages 30-40 feet thick.

At New Cumberland, there are both Lower Kittanning and Middle Kittanning coal and clay seams. Clay seams under Middle Kittanning coal had flint-like properties and are known as fire clays. This clay, Middle Kittanning, is primarily used for building brick and paving brick. The Lower Kittanning clay is primarily used for sewer pipe and low and intermediate heat duty flue tile.

Lower and Middle Kittanning clays have been mixed together along with blue and gray shale to make paving brick as well to achieve a higher degree of durability. These clays also have flint-like properties and are used to make refractory bricks that are used to line steel ladles in the steel industry.

Clarion clay is predominately fire clay and is sometimes associated with Lower Kittanning coal. There is not that much of this type of clay in West Virginia. Clarion clay is considered the most valuable in the quadrangles and was mined on the east side of the Allegheny River. The clay was used for front brick fireproofing and sewer pipe, which is the principle product. The sewer pipe was glazed at a temperature of 2,700 degrees and will withstand 3,000 degrees.

Nearly all mines that produced clay for brick manufacturing in and near New Cumberland were of the fire clay property.

Kittanning and Clarion fire clays are represented on the right (rectangle) for Pennsylvania and left (square) for the West Virginia panhandle. Keep in mind that these Kittanning and Clarion coal and clay seams are predominated throughout West Virginia especially along both banks of the Ohio River.

Mack Manufacturing Company – See section after Glossary

Martin Brick Making Machine – Developed and produced by Henry Martin. This machine allowed clay to enter the cavity while a Corliss engine was attached to create a rotation. This rotation caused the clay to be pressed into bricks at the bottom.

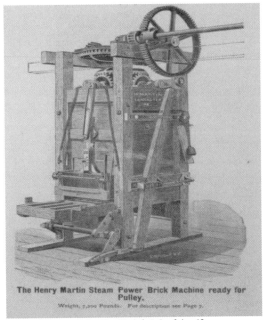

The Henry Martin Steam Power Brick Machine ready for Pulley.
Weight, 7,300 Pounds. For description see Page 7.

Henry Martin Brick Machine[12]

220

Means Press – Means presses were also used in brickyards, but little is known about this type of press. Google searches revealed nothing with that name.

Moulding[6] – A term used in brickmaking that referred to molding of the brick. It is unclear why the "u" was added to the word. Before the invention of the steam-driven machines, bricks were moulded (molded) by hand. The assistant brick moulder was called the "clot" moulder, and he would prepare a lump of clay and give it to the brick moulder. The brick moulder was the key to the operation and was the head of the team. He would stand at the moulding table for twelve to fourteen hours a day, and with the help of his assistants could make 3500 to 5000 bricks per day. He would take the clot of clay, roll it in sand, and "dash" it into the sanded mould. The clay was pressed into the mould by hand, and the excess clay was removed from the top of the mould with a strike, which was a flat stick that had been soaking in water. This excess clay was returned to the clot moulder to be reformed. Sand was used to prevent the clay from sticking to the mould.

Single, double, four, or six brick moulds were used. The single brick mould had an advantage in that a worker could carry it to the drying area.

Pugmill[20] – A pugmill or pug mill is a machine in which clay or other materials are mixed into a plastic state prior to being inserted into a brickmaking machine. In today's terms, it would be a large mixing machine.

Raymond Equipment[7] – Raymond equipment was manufactured by the CW Raymond Company in Dayton, Ohio, in the 1860's and was exclusively used in brickmaking. Their equipment consisted of brickmaking machines, crushers (clay & shale), augers, presses and represses, and pipe presses.

However, the company went into bankruptcy and had to close in 1914 because some brick companies were not able to pay for the equipment they had purchased.

RAYMOND No. 1 DAYTONIAN BRICK MACHINE AND TRIUMPH CUTTING TABLE.

SHOWING No. 1 Brick Machine and Triumph Side-Cut Cutting Table, with separating belt. A practical combination of machine and table for plants of ordinary size. Capacity 3,000 to 4,000 American standard size bricks per hour. The brick can be easily handled from the separating belt to the feeding table of the Re-press.

Raymond brickmaking machine 1890, which is capable of 3000 to 4000 bricks per hour

Richardson Machine[8] – Nathaniel Adams of Newburgh & Cornwell, NY, initially invented the first brickmaking machine in 1830. This particular moulding machine was manual in nature requiring humans or animals (mules or horses) to operate. Richard Ver Valen developed a brickmaking machine in 1852 which became known as the Richardson Machine. This machine was connected to a steam-powered drive shaft called a "powerline." This created the ability to make thousands more bricks per day.

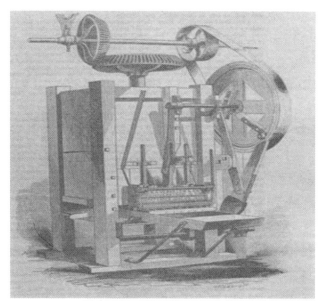

Richardson Machine 1852

Roll[10] – A "roll" is a sandstone thickening of the roof that causes the clay seam to thin out. This is evident in the map below of the Rockyside mine. See the "roll" and how all the seams stop at the roll.

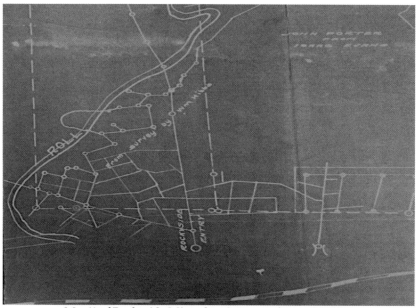

Map[11] *of Rockyside Mine showing a sandstone "Roll"*

Rolls[14] – Rolls are also used for crushing the clay and should not be confused with the word roll (for sandstone). After the clay is mined, it was wheeled or pulled to the "rolls" where it was ground and reground until it was of sufficient fineness. These rolls are also called "crushers" or "clappers" that crush or clap the clay to a chunkier consistence. Rolls were primarily used for getting the clay to a fine consistency. Once it was of the desired consistency, the clay was then taken to the wet pan where it was mixed with water.

Turner Vaughn & Taylor Press[9] – The Turner Vaughn & Taylor Press was invented in 1856 and made exclusively for producing sewer pipe.

In 1869, The Turner Vaughn & Taylor Co placed a 36 x 18 inch double clay cylinder steam press in Freeman Brothers plant at Freeman Station on the Ohio River. This was the first steam press in the Ohio River territory for making sewer pipe.

A Turner Vaughn & Taylor Press used to make sewer pipe[15]

Vitrified Bricks – Vitrified bricks are used in construction of buildings. They are produced when wet clay bricks are exposed to excessive heat during the firing process, sintering the surface of the brick and forming a shiny, dark-colored coating. Vitrified brick is resistant to water and chemicals.

Wet Pan[21] – Wet pan or wet pans were similar in design to pug mill machinery. They were classified as large mixing machines to mix the clay and shale to the proper consistency.

Zalia - This area of Hancock County still exists on maps and is considered to be between Holberts Run Road and Rainy Hill Road, just north of the Kings Creek Bridge. It would be a distance of about one and three quarters of a mile south of New Cumberland.

Glossary of Terms References

1. Clay Working – The *Brick and Clay Record* – Volumes 32 and 33, pages 60 & 61
2. Corliss Steam Engine – *Wikipedia.org/wiki/*Corliss Steam engine
3. Cyrus Chambers – www.google.com/patents/US240886
4. Eu Daly Kilns – www.google.com/patents/US508003
5. Kittanning Clay – *U.S. Geological Survey*, Issue 279, page 166
6. Moulding – *The Clay-Worker* Volume 61-62, page 192
7. Raymond Equipment – *History of the City of Dayton and Montgomery County, Ohio*, Volume 1, page 659/660
8. Richardson Machine – Hudson River Brickmaking – Brickcollecting.com
9. Turner Vaughn & Taylor Press – *The Clay-Record*, Volume 25-26, page 34
10. *Glossary of Terms Used in Coal Mining* – 1923
11. Mine Map – *Map of Mack MFG Co. Mines W.Va.* – June 25, 1923 prepared by James E. Kelley – Joe Juszczak
12. *Brick Machinery Illustrated Catalogue* – Henry Martin – 1886
13. *Civil Engineering Handbook (Allis Mineral System Grinding Division)* Svedala Industries, Inc. – page 20
14. *The Clay Worker* Volume 70, page 112
15. *The Brick and Clay Record*, Volume 9, page 58
16. www.madehow.org/brick-making, 1850-1875
17. *The Brick and Clay Record, Volume 12, page 47*
18. *The Brick and Clay Record, Volume 12, page 52*
19. *The Brick, Volume 23, page 134*
20. https://en.wikipedia.org/wiki/pugmill
21. https://en.wikipedia.org/wiki/wetpan
22. encyclopedia2.the freedictionary.com/vitrified+brick

Mack Manufacturing Company Overview

In 1894, the Mack Manufacturing Company of Philadelphia, PA, purchased all brickyard assets from Captain John Porter. Those assets included Sligo, Clifton, Crescent, Etna, Eagle, Union, and Rockyside brickyard and sewer pipe plants. Our research uncovered an original pricing guide/brochure from early 1900 that reflects the products that could be purchased. It is only appropriate to include photos from the book to illustrate the variety of unique products that were made. There were a variety of measuring charts that included; carrying capacity of sewer pipe, directions for laying sewer pipe, measuring for flue liners, and various tables showing water pressures at different elevations and weight of material for each foot of depth when building with brick or stone.

All photos shown courtesy of Mack Manufacturing Company

Mack Sales Book for the Customer Product Selections
Book photos courtsey of Mack Manufacturing

MACK MANUFACTURING CO.

AMERICA'S STANDARD VITRIFIED BRICK AND BLOCK
FOR
STREET PAVING

Of the Many Advantages in Favor of Vitrified Brick and Block Pavements

They stand first, as to Cheapness of Construction
" Economy of Maintenance
" Facility of Repairs
" Freedom from Decay
" Healthfulness
" Foothold for Horses

Equal to any other material as to
Water-tight Cover
Freedom from Noise
Freedom from Dust
Ease of Traction

Under our skillful manipulation our product has steadily improved in quality, and to-day we stand at the head of the market in this industry, justly entitled to the distinction of being the manufacturers of AMERICA'S LEADING VITRIFIED PAVING BRICK.

Brick pavements have been used in different parts of Europe for over a century. In this country the first was laid in Charleston, W. Va., about twenty-five years ago, and were so successful that brick has gradually been adopted in over three hundred of our cities and towns.

There have been all kinds of brick used—good, bad and indifferent—since the first brick pavement was laid, and this has resulted in disappointment in many places where other than a suitable grade of brick has been used.

Brick for paving must combine toughness with vitrification, and to produce such a brick requires clay of certain properties, and a thorough knowledge of the business on the part of the manufacturer. There are many clays that will burn to a condition of vitrification, but lack toughness, and are, therefore, inferior in quality for paving purposes.

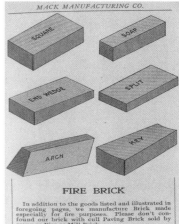

MACK MANUFACTURING CO.

FIRE BRICK

In addition to the goods listed and illustrated in foregoing pages, we manufacture Brick made especially for fire purposes. Please don't confound our brick with cull Paving Brick sold by many as Fire or Mill Brick.

As is well known, the New Cumberland Fire Clay is of a very superior quality, and we have no hesitation in guaranteeing our Brick as eminently suitable and satisfactory for all ordinary purposes.

We have 75 kilns at our various works and have naturally made a study of this subject with the view of securing the best and most economical results in actual service, hence we are justified in claiming more than ordinary experience, besides having thoroughly tested our clay in every conceivable manner.

For places where extra high quality (known as No. 1) Brick are required, we shall be pleased to furnish estimates on receipt of request with information as to character of service required from the Brick.

Prices on these goods quoted on application.

MACK MANUFACTURING CO.

Trade ◄ MACK MANUF'G CO. ► Mark

Recognizing the demand for a superior quality of Vitrified Glazed Sewer Pipe, no effort or expense has been spared to make our "DIAMOND" brand second to none in the market .. .. .. With an enlarged capacity for production and unexcelled shipping facilities, we submit the present price-list in the full confidence of our ability to execute orders with promptness and to the entire satisfaction of our patrons .. .. ..

Trade ◄ MACK MANUF'G CO. ► Mark

Inside pages from Mack Sales Book
Book photos courtsey of Mack Manufacturing

228

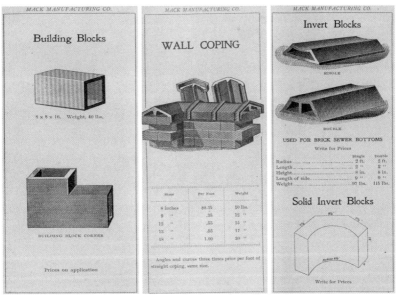

Mack Building Blocks and Wall Coping
Book photos courtsey of Mack Manufacturing

Mack Chimney Tops
Book photos courtsey of Mack Manufacturing

229

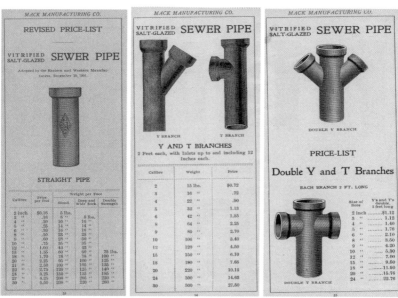

Mack Sewer Pipe and Pricing Guide
Book photos courtsey of Mack Manufacturing

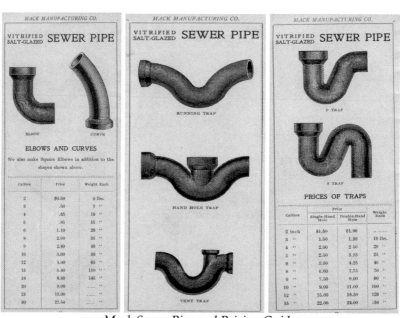

Mack Sewer Pipe and Pricing Guides
Book photos courtsey of Mack Manufacturing

Mack Reducers, Pricing, and Information Guide
Book photos courtsey of Mack Manufacturing

Mack Flue Liners and Stove Pipe with Pricing
Book photos courtsey of Mack Manufacturing

About the Authors

Thomas W. Zielinsky was born in Steubenville, Ohio, on December 28, 1946, and was raised in New Cumberland, West Virginia. He is the oldest of three sons born to Walda A. (Zumer) and Walter A. Zielinsky. Thomas graduated from Oak Glen High School in 1964 and attended West Virginia University for two years studying Electrical Engineering. He left school and enlisted in the United States Army in 1966 and was honorably discharged in 1969. Having served during the Vietnam War era, he was a member of the Air Defense Artillery Nike Hercules Missile unit, 100th Artillery Group, 5th Region Air Defense Command, where he achieved the rank of Specialist 5 – E5. After leaving the Army, he worked as an electronic technician for General Dynamics Electronics Division in Rochester, New York, on the F-111-F series fighter jet.

Leaving New York, he was hired by Weirton Steel Corporation in 1970 as a general laborer. In 1974 he was transferred to the Strip Steel Department as a salaried Electronic Systems Engineer on the No. 9 Tandem Mill.

He held a number of different senior management positions and ultimately became Senior Director in 1999 until his retirement at the end of March 2004.

Hired by the Hancock County Commission in 2006 as Executive Director Technology and Communications, he had responsibilities for Emergency Management, 911 Center, and all computer and network systems within the courthouse. He retired in 2013.

He holds degrees in Electronic Engineering, Computer Science, and a Masters in Business Administration.

He resides in Weirton, WV, with his wife Patty. They have four children between them and 10 grandchildren. In his spare time, he is a professional musician playing the Concerto accordion.

He is the author of *The Final Days of Weirton Steel* published in 2010. This will be the author's second book.

George B. Hines III was born in 1951 in Steubenville, Ohio, the eldest son of Ramona "Boots" Hines of New Cumberland and the late George Hines, Jr., of Weirton. He attended school in New Cumberland and graduated from Oak Glen High School in 1969. In 1971, while working at Weirton Steel Company, he was drafted into the US Army and served for two years in Texas before being honorably discharged in 1973. While in the army he trained as a senior gunner with the 1st Cavalry Air Defense Air Mobile Artillery.

After his discharge, he returned to Weirton Steel where he worked in the boiler house until his retirement in 2002. Later that same year he took a job working for the city of New Cumberland as its community service director and the chairman of Keep New Cumberland Beautiful. A life-long history buff, he co-authored a book on the history of Hancock County and started a local history museum at the New Cumberland City Building featuring numerous photos and memorabilia from the area. He continues his work with beautification by maintaining two parks and several flower gardens in the city as well as serving as the president of the New Cumberland Garden Club and a board member of the Magic Tree Community Garden.

George and his wife Milli are the parents of two sons, George and Phil, and the grandparents of one granddaughter, Sophie. They live in the home George built on his wife's family farm near New Manchester. When he isn't working, George enjoys traveling and spending quality time with his granddaughter.

This will be the author's second co-authored book.

Index

237

Phillips, Matthew 13, 16, 83, 244
Phillips, Minnie 83
Porter Brick Company 18, 43
Porter Children 101
Porter Company 11, 18, 43, 47
Porter, Eliza (Spratt) 101
Porter, Frederick Gregg 101
Porter, J. Nessley 101
Porter, James iii, 11-14, 33, 43, 44, 101, 104
Porter, John 12-15, 30, 85, 97-102, 106, 227, 243
Porter, John Chester 101
Porter, Josephine 101
Porter, Mary Elizabeth 102
Porter, Moses 97, 101
Porter, Robert 13
Porter, William 13-14, 44, 106
Porter, William Keefer 101
Porter and Beall 43, 46
Porter's 97, 210
Powers, Lenora 131
Powers, Ray 131

R

Reese 28, 74
Reese, Bobby 141, 143
Reese, Butch 143
Reese, Clarence 131
Reese, Ed viii, 28, 131, 143, 175, 176
Reese, James, Josephine, Gertrude, Marjorie 90
Reese, Kenny 143
Reese, Patty viii, 141, 143
Reese, Robert (Dink) 143
Reese, Saraha 131
Reese (Zumer), Josephine 129
Richardson, John 193
Riggi, Pam ix, 75
Riggi, Pam & Vito ix
Robb 74
Robb, George 214
Robb, J. W. 193

Robb, John T. 14
Robertson 74
Roefaro, John 132
Roefaro, Eleanor (Straight) 132
Roseberry 74
Ryan, Ethel, Lawrence 7

S

Salisberry 28
Salisberry, Frank 131
Schiavoni, Vince ix, 86, 87, 106, 199, 201
Servall, A. N 15
Shane, F. 14
Shanley 12
Shawl 11
Shepard, Clara 143
Shepard, Buzzy 143
Simon, Lucas 196
Smith, B. J. 13
Smith, Jeremiah 12
Smith, Porter & Company iii, iv, 12, 13
Sprague, Harry 193, 214
Spilecki 28
Spilecki, Chet & Alex 140
Spilecki, Chet & Doris 140
Spilecki, Wanda ix, 140
Spilitsky, Gregory 71
Staley 74
Staley, Dick 214
Steveson, T. C 16
Stewart 74
Stewart, Dora 192
Stewart Farm 5
Stewart, Joseph 12, 13
Stolarchick, 61
Stolarchick, Joseph 67, 71
Stolarczyk 28, 61, 67, 141
Stolarczyk, Emily 141
Stolarczyk, Joseph, Mary, Darlene, Josephine, Sophie, Teddy, Emily, Virginia, Helene 90
Stolarczyk, Joe 196

Brickyards north of New Cumberland

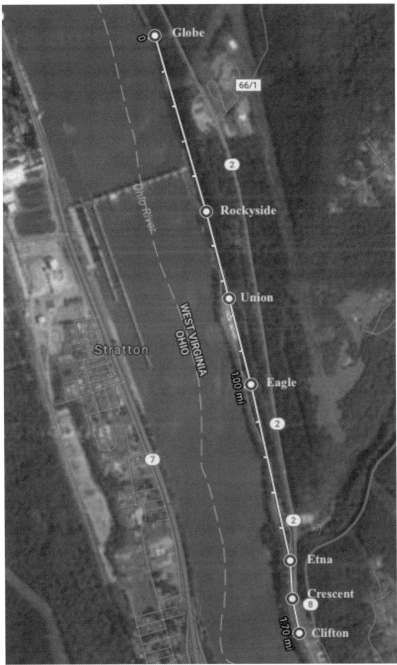

Photo of Mack Manufacturing brickyards
Photo courtesy of Google Maps

Brickyards south of New Cumberland

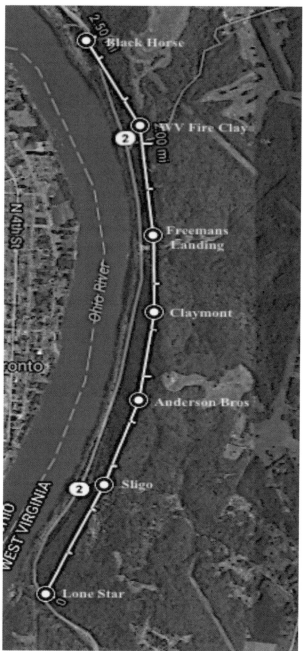

Photo courtesy of Google Maps

New Cumberland Key Events Timeline 1784 – 1980

Year	Key Event
1784	Cuppytown – New Cumberland's first name
1830	Kittanning Fire Clay found near Holberts Run
1832	Freeman's Brickyard started near Holberts Run
1834	Claymont Brickyard started 1.5 miles south of NC
1836	Clifton Brickyard Lower Works started north of NC
1837	Lone Star Brickyard started north of Kings Creek
1837	Sligo Brickyard started north of Lone Star
1837	Anderson Brickyard started north of Sligo
1839	New Cumberland established by John Cuppy
1840	Small un-named brickyard started in Deep Gut Run
1844	Aetna & Cunningham started north of NC
1845	Black Horse started south of NC
1846	Two small brickyards started on Hardins Run
1848	Hancock County became organized on January 15
1851	Chapman Foundry started operations
1856	Daily mail service commenced for NC
1856	Crescent Middle & Upper started north of NC
1858	Crescent Brickyard started as Crescent
1862	Gas well struck in Deep Gut Run
1868	Union Brickyard started north of NC
1870	Eagle and Rockyside Brickyards started north - NC
1871	Crescent merged with Clifton Works
1872	New Cumberland incorporated by WV Legislation
1874	Standard Fire Brick started Globe Brickyard
1875	Freeman Brickyard expands farther south
1876	Gas first used as fuel for brickmaking in kilns
1880	Cunningham & Taylor started north of NC
1881	Cunningham plants destroyed by fire – not rebuilt
1882	First brick street laid in New Cumberland
1884	New Cumberland settled as county seat
1884	John Porter laid brick on Third Street, Steubenville
1887	Marshall house built by Oliver Sheridan
1889	Chelsea China started
1889	American Sewer Pipe purchased Black Horse
1890	Etna, Union and Eagle sold to John Porter
1893	John Porter purchases 35 acres near Newell

1894	Brickyards except Globe sold - Mack Manufacturing
1894	Chelsea China hit by major fire
1897	McElfresh Clay started south of NC
1897	Freeman Brickyard expands farther south
1898	West Virginia Fire Clay started in operation
1900	Etna Brickyard destroyed by fire – later rebuilt
1901	Acme (Chapman) Clay works established
1904	First Catholic Church built on Rockyside
1904	Lock & Dam No. 9 construction began
1904	Chelsea China Company sold to Union Potteries
1904	Clifton, Sligo & Eagle brickyards shut down
1906	Globe Brickyard destroyed by fire – never rebuilt
1906	Mack Company opens general store – People's store
1907	Etna Brickyard destroyed by fire but later rebuilt
1907	Chelsea China destroyed by fire
1909	New Globe Brickyard started outside of Newell
1911	Union Brickyard destroyed by fire but later rebuilt
1914	Lock & Dam No.9 was completed
1916	Duraloy Company being built
1916	Mack deposes all brickyards to Wheeling Capital
1917	Old Clifton building & coal bins destroyed by fire
1921	Catholic School started in NC
1924	Crescent Brick Company started by W. A. Bonitz
1926	D. D. Moses purchases Crescent Brick from Bonitz
1929	Hancock Manufacturing began operations
1930	New Cumberland Glass Company destroyed by fire
1937	Duraloy Plant was destroyed by fire – never rebuilt
1944	Chapman Foundry purchased by Matthew Phillips
1952	Phillips Lumber and Supply was founded
1955	New Lock & Dam project started in Stratton, OH
1961	New Lock & Dam project completed
1963	West Virginia Fire Clay closed its operations
1970	New Cumberland Metals Products was sold
1979	Crescent Brick sealed the Hardins Run Mine
1980	Union Brick of Crescent Brick ceased operations